ARISTOTLE ON EMOTION

ARISTOTLE ON EMOTION

A contribution to
philosophical psychology,
rhetoric, poetics,
politics and ethics

W. W. Fortenbaugh

BARNES & NOBLE
BOOKS
10 East 53d St., New York 10022
(a division of Harper & Row Publishers, Inc.)

Published in the U.S.A. 1975 by
HARPER & ROW PUBLISHERS, INC.
BARNES & NOBLE IMPORT DIVISION

ISBN 0-06-492168-9

Printed in Great Britain by
Ebenezer Baylis and Son Limited
The Trinity Press, Worcester, and London

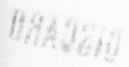

CONTENTS

TO MY PARENTS

PREFACE

At the very outset I wish to acknowledge the enormous help I have received from many different people. I cannot begin to thank them all by name, but I can say that their assistance has been invaluable and hopefully will be returned over the years ahead. There are, however, two persons whose support has been so extraordinarily generous that I feel no hesitation in singling them out for special mention. The first is the late Glenn Morrow, my former teacher and counsellor. He contributed significantly to the early development of views expressed in this book. I am only sad that he died before publication and therefore did not live to receive the formal thanks of this acknowledgment. The second person is Richard Sorabji. He worked with me through the later stages of creation, offering innumerable constructive criticisms and, when needed, the warm support of a sympathetic friend.

I have also benefited significantly from several generous grants. In 1967–8, I had the privilege of being a Junior Fellow at the Center for Hellenic Studies, where I began serious work on the topic of this book. In 1972–3 I enjoyed a Study Fellowship provided by the American Council of Learned Societies and thereby found time to bring my work close to completion. My thanks are extended to both these institutions and to the National Endowment for the Humanities and the Rutgers Research Council who also supported me along the way.

In writing this book I have occasionally drawn upon previously published material. I thank the editor of *Arethusa* and the de Gruyter Verlag for permission to reproduce several pages, and at the same time I must alert the reader familiar with my earlier publications that I am not committed to defending the past in its entirety. Criticism and reflection have inevitably led to modification, not to say abandonment, of certain previously held views and arguments.

Finally, I thank my wife and children for living with the frustrations of creation. Their patience was too often demanded and too rarely acknowledged.

Douglass College, Rutgers University   W.W.F.
January 1974

CHAPTER ONE

Aristotle's Analysis of Emotional Response

1. Emotion and cognition

During the period of Aristotle's residence in Plato's Academy an investigation of emotion was undertaken which was to have profound effects upon the subsequent course of philosophical psychology, rhetoric, poetics and political and ethical theory. Members of the Academy including Aristotle focused upon emotions as distinct from bodily sensations and bodily drives and tried to explain the involvement of cognition in emotional response. A satisfactory explanation was not immediately forthcoming. We can observe Plato wrestling with this problem in his *Philebus* and can catch echoes of Academic discussion in Aristotle's *Topics*. But when an answer was developed and incorporated by Aristotle within his *Rhetoric*, the consequences were of considerable and lasting significance. Emotional appeal acquired a new dignity within rhetorical theory, dramatic poetry was freed from Platonic charges of corrupting reason, a new moral psychology was developed and a variety of problems within the sphere of politics and ethics received a new interpretation. Some of these developments are well known, but others are not. Certainly the several developments have not been brought together and their combined importance has not been emphasised. Accordingly I wish to fill a significant gap by recounting in some detail how Aristotle and other members of the Academy came to grips with emotional response as a psychological, rhetorical, poetic, political and ethical phenomenon. My account will cut across fields of philosophical interest, but it will not be complicated and in the end should help us to appreciate properly the full significance of Aristotle's interest in emotional response.

We may take our start from Plato's *Philebus*, a dialogue which presents the competing claims of pleasure and wisdom to be the psychic state or condition which is able to make a man's life blessed ($11^{d}4–9$). Socrates champions wisdom over pleasure, and while he does not show wisdom to be the good, he wins the day by showing

9

it superior to pleasure. What especially interests us is that in the course of this dialogue Socrates distinguishes between three kinds of mixed pleasures and pains: those mixtures which concern the body and are found in the body, those that belong to the soul itself and are found in the soul, and those that belong to the soul and to the body ($46^b8-{}^c2$). Mixed bodily pleasures and pains are illustrated by simultaneous sensations of hot and cold and by itches and tickles combined with the soothing effect of rubbing and scratching (46^c6-47^a1). Mixed pleasures and pains belonging to body and soul are illustrated by cases of depletion such as the condition of hungry and thirsty men who not only experience painful bodily sensations but also enjoy the expectation of replenishment ($47^c3-{}^d3$). Finally, mixed pleasures and pains belonging to the soul alone are explained by an illustrative list: anger, fear, longing, lament, love, emulation and envy (47^e1-2, cf. $50^b7-{}^c1$) and by a lengthy discussion of the mixed feelings of envious individuals (48^b8-50^a9). The importance of this classification is to be seen in the bringing together of emotional responses into a single class marked off from other kinds of mixed pleasures and pains that depend upon certain bodily conditions. Socrates is clear that anger and fear are fundamentally different from itches and tickles and hungers and thirsts, that emotional responses are neither bodily sensations nor bodily drives and therefore are to be grouped separately as pleasures and pains of the soul itself (47^e2-3).

However, Socrates is not altogether clear concerning the cognitive nature of emotional response. This is an important point deserving close attention. When the interlocutor Protarchus balks at calling pleasure and pain true or false, Socrates is compelled to discuss the relationship of cognition to emotion and other kinds of pains and pleasures. Protarchus is ready to concede that opinion can be true or false, but he is not ready to admit that pleasure and pain, fear and expectation can be called true or false ($36^c6-{}^d2$). At first Socrates endeavours to win over Protarchus by pointing out similarities between opinion and pleasure and pain. The argument runs smoothly enough until Socrates tries to establish that pleasures and pains are like opinion in that they can be mistaken. To establish this, Socrates argues that pleasures often occur together with false opinion (37^e10). The use of 'with' is unfortunate. Protarchus construes this preposition as simple concurrence and thinks of opinion as something which accompanies but is external to pleasure.

He therefore objects that in such a case the opinion would be false but no one would call the pleasure false (37ᵉ12–38ᵃ2). Socrates compliments Protarchus on this objection and then presses on. He speaks of pleasure and pain following true and false opinion (38ᵇ9) and undertakes a more exhaustive study of opinion and its relationship to pleasure and pain. He gives a graphic description of our thought processes and finally argues that just as opinions may lack a basis in reality, so pleasures and pains may be without grounds (40ᵈ8). And what is true of pleasure and pain in general is, of course, true of painful emotions such as fear, anger and the like. They may be without foundation and said to be false (40ᵉ2–4). Protarchus agrees and does not object when Socrates says that true and false opinions fill up pleasures and pains with their own affection (42ᵃ7–9). Opinion is so intimately connected with pleasure and pain that it can infect them with its own condition.

The *Philebus* certainly makes clear that Plato saw an intimate relationship between emotion and cognition. But it fails to make this relationship clear. The preposition 'with' (37ᵉ10) only gets Socrates into trouble. The verb 'follows' (38ᵇ9) needs qualification, and the verb 'fills up' (42ᵃ9) is at best a metaphor which avoids the problem without solving it. Further clarification was necessary. This is indicated dramatically by Socrates' promise to continue the discussion tomorrow (50ᵈ8–ᵉ1) and we can imagine lively debate within the Academy concerning the way in which cognition is involved in emotional response. Aristotle was most certainly part of this debate and in the *Topics* we can see him drawing upon it for illustrative purposes. Both pain and the thought of outrage are said to be essential to the emotion of anger, for the angry man is pained and thinks himself outraged. But in what way is the thought of outrage essential to anger? Apparently it is not the genus of anger, since pain is a more likely candidate and is not the genus (127ᵇ26–32). Nor can we say without further clarification that anger is pain 'with' the thought of outrage. The ambiguity of this preposition is clear in the *Philebus* (37ᵉ10) and spelled out in the *Topics* where we are told that in the case of anger the preposition 'with' should not be construed as 'and' or 'made up out of' or 'in the same receptacle' or 'in the same place' or 'in the same time' but rather in terms of causal connection. Anger is pain with the thought of outrage in the sense of pain on account of (*dia*) such a thought (150ᵇ27–151ᵃ19). The *Topics* prefers a causal definition (cf. 156ᵃ32–

33) and in this preference looks forward to Aristotle's own analysis set forth in the *Rhetoric*.[1]

In the second book of the *Rhetoric* Aristotle defines anger as a desire for revenge accompanied by pain on account of (*dia*) an apparent slight to oneself or to one's own, the slight being unjustified (1378ª30–2). This definition involves a peculiarly Aristotelian answer to Academic debate. Making use of his own logical tools Aristotle construes the thought of outrage as the efficient cause mentioned in the essential definition. Anger is not a pain which happens to occur together with (*meta*) the thought of outrage. On the contrary, anger is necessarily caused by the thought of outrage, so that such a thought is mentioned in the essential definition of anger. The same is true of fear. It is caused by the thought of imminent danger, so that the appearance of future evil, destructive or painful, is mentioned in the definition of anger (1382ª21–2). Fear is not some pain or bodily disturbance distinct from cognition. It is a complex phenomenon which necessarily involves not only painful disturbance but also the thought of danger.

This is Aristotle's answer to an Academic puzzle and one which is a striking anticipation of much modern controversy. By insisting on the essential involvement of cognition in emotional response Aristotle has rejected the view of James that emotion is properly a bodily sensation and aligned himself with Bedford in opposition to Pitcher, who thinks cognitions characteristic of but not essential to emotional response.[2] For Aristotle the thought of outrage and the thought of impending danger are not merely characteristic of anger and fear respectively. They are necessary and properly mentioned in the essential definitions of anger and fear.

2. *The study of emotion and demonstrative science*

Aristotle's analysis of emotion is of interest not only in that it offers a solution to Academic debate and looks forward to modern

---

[1] It is quite possible that the analysis of emotion set forth in the *Rhetoric* was preceded and prepared for by an earlier analysis which formed part of Aristotle's now lost *Diaireseis*. On this possibility see below, p. 29 n. 1.

[2] W. James, *The Principles of Psychology* (New York 1890) 2.449. E. Bedford, 'Emotions', *Proceedings of the Aristotelian Society* 57 (1956–7) 281–304, reprinted in D. Gustafson (ed.), *Essays in Philosophical Psychology* (Garden City 1964) 77–98. G. Pitcher, 'Emotion', *Mind* 74 (1965) 326–46.

controversy. It is also of interest in that it brings the study of emotions within the framework of demonstrative science as explained in the *Posterior Analytics*. By building the efficient cause into the definition of individual emotions Aristotle was conforming to his own principle that questions of essence and questions of cause are one and the same (90ᵃ14–15, 31–2, 93ᵃ3–4). What is an eclipse? It is a deprivation of light from the moon by the obstruction of the earth. And what is the cause of an eclipse or why does the moon suffer eclipse? Because light fails owing to the obstruction of the earth (90ᵃ15–18). For Aristotle knowing the essence of an eclipse involves knowing the efficient cause (98ᵇ21–4). Similarly with emotions knowing the essence involves being able to give a definition that 'shows why' (93ᵇ38). Only with emotions the task is considerably easier. For the cause is not an elusive object of astronomical research. Aristotle prefers to explain lunar eclipses by reference to the interposition of the earth. But he recognises interposition as only one of three possible causes, the other two being rotation and extinction (93ᵇ5–6). To choose between such cases it would do no good to ask ordinary Greeks how they conceive of lunar eclipses. For the cause was not part of their everyday notion of eclipse and in any event was still a matter of controversy among experts. Certainty demanded an advance in astronomical investigation or a miraculous trip to the moon from where the interposition of the earth would be obvious (90ᵃ27–30). This is not the case with emotions. Were an ordinary Greek asked what fear is, he would more than likely give an answer which mentioned the thought of imminent danger. Indeed Aristotle tells us that they, that is to say ordinary men, define fear as an expectation of evil (*EN* 1115ᵃ9). To give a causal definition of fear it was not necessary to add information in the way that the cause had to be discovered and added to the everyday notion of eclipse. Rather it was necessary to tighten up or make precise what was already implicit in everyday notions of fear, anger and other emotions.

Aristotle did this in accordance with his conception of scientific method. He recognised cognition as the efficient cause and formulated a demonstrative account of emotional response. The idea of offering a syllogistic explanation of angry behaviour is clearly present in the *Posterior Analytics* where Aristotle illustrates how the efficient cause is exhibited through the middle term of a syllogism. Why, he asks, did war befall the Athenians? Because they attacked

Sardis. Let A stand for war, B stand for unprovoked aggression and C stand for the Athenians. B (unprovoked aggression) applies to C (the Athenians) and A (war) applies to B (unprovoked aggression). The middle term is the efficient cause ($94^a36–^b8$). Replace 'war' with 'anger' and 'unprovoked aggression' with 'apparent insult' and we obtain a more general explanation appropriate to all kinds of angry response. But the procedure of demonstrative science is preserved. Emotional response is explained syllogistically and the efficient cause is treated as the middle term.

Including the thought of outrage among the essential components of anger has the necessary consequence that a man cannot be angry when he thinks himself treated justly ($1380^b16–18$). It has two further consequences which merit special mention. First, it enables Aristotle to argue that an angry man is necessarily angry at some individual like Cleon ($1378^a33–4$). Aristotle's reasoning is clear enough. Anger is directed at some individual, because anger involves thought or belief about some outrageous individual. Beliefs have objects and, since beliefs are a necessary ingredient in anger, it follows that angry men are necessarily enraged at someone or other.[1] This point was, of course, implicit in Greek language and literature before Aristotle. We may refer to Thucydides who tells us that when Pericles saw that the Athenians were exasperated by their situation and angry at (*es* 2.60.1, *es* or *ep'* 2.65.1) him, because they held him responsible for leading them into war (2.59.2, 60.4,7), he called an assembly and tried by speaking to alter their emotion (2.65.1). Here it is implied that an emotion like anger is directed at a person because of a belief concerning the person. But it is not explicit and does not seem to have been made explicit

---

[1] In saying that an angry man is necessarily angry at some individual like Cleon ($1378^a33–4$) or Callias or Socrates ($1382^a5–6$), Aristotle is not claiming that an angry man must be able to name or identify the particular individual who insulted him. Clearly a man can be angry at whoever insulted him even though he has not (as yet) found out precisely who is responsible for the insult. Aristotle is not unaware of this. His point is simply that anger cannot be directed against either man in general (1378^a34) or some class of men such as thieves or informers ($1382^a6–7$). For anger is due to personal insult (1378^a31, 1382^a3) which is a particular act perpetrated by a particular agent. This agent may be thought of quite vaguely as the (perhaps still unknown) perpetrator of personal insult, or alternatively he may be thought of quite specifically as Cleon, Callias or Socrates, but in neither case would it be correct to say that anger is directed against a class of men or man in general.

until Aristotle brought the study of emotion within the framework of demonstrative science.

The second consequence is that Aristotle was able to make clear the difference between anger and a similar emotion like hate. By building the thought of personal insult into the essence of anger Aristotle could draw a logical distinction between this emotion and the emotion of hate. For the occurrence of hate it is not necessary to believe in personal outrage. It is only necessary to think of someone as a certain kind of person—for example, a thief or sycophant (1382ª3–7). In other words the efficient cause became a powerful tool for distinguishing the logical boundaries between related emotions. Both fear and shame involve disturbance (1382ª21, 1383ᵇ13) and both can be labelled *phobos* (cf. *EN* 1128ᵇ11). But they are essentially different in that fear necessarily involves the thought of impending harm (1382ª21–2), while shame necessarily involves the thought of disgrace (1383ᵇ13–18, 1384ª22).

It would be, of course, a mistake to think that Aristotle only concerned himself with the efficient cause of emotional response. Indeed, focusing exclusively upon one kind of cause would be a departure from scientific method. Aristotle is interested in definitions that facilitate demonstration and therefore is prepared to criticise 'empty' definitions which do not contain the items necessary for deductive explanations (*De An.* 402ᵇ25–403ª2).[1] In regard to emotions this means that he will prefer definitions which mention more than the thought which moves a man to respond emotionally. Anger is not to be defined by the efficient cause alone. Mention must also be made of the material and final causes, that is to say of blood boiling around the heart and a desire for returning pain (*De An.* 403ª25–ᵇ2). The inclusion of boiling blood in the essential definition makes possible a demonstrative explanation of why angry men become hot and turn red. The inclusion of returning pain or taking revenge prepares the way for a similar explanation of various kinds of goal-directed behaviour. Moreover, the mention of returning pain has the effect of tying anger to action and therefore marking it off from an emotion like shame which is not necessarily tied to any particular kind of action. With this distinction we shall be concerned later when we consider moral virtue in relation to practical and non-practical emotions (Chapter Four, Section 4).

[1] Cf. R. R. K. Sorabji, 'Aristotle and Oxford Philosophy', *American Philosophical Quarterly* 6 (1969) 130.

At this moment we need only be clear that Aristotle's analysis of emotional response is an inclusive analysis which treats emotion as a complex phenomenon. It makes room for a variety of items within the essential definition of an individual emotion and therefore makes possible a variety of demonstrative explanations that would not be possible with a less richly packed definition. For Aristotle this is good scientific method.

3. *A contribution to rhetoric*

Aristotle's deductive analysis of emotion was of considerable importance for rhetoric. Within the Academy Plato had criticised severely current rhetorical methods and had called for a new and philosophical rhetoric. If rhetoric was to be taught in the Academy, it had to acquire some measure of scientific method. Towards this end, Aristotle imposed a demonstrative method both upon his discussion of particular premises in Book I and upon his discussion of emotions in Book II.[1] For example, in the first book Aristotle introduces a definition of goodness with the technical term 'let-it-be' (*estô*).[2] He pauses to clarify two words, resumes with the phrase 'these things having been laid down' and then proceeds to draw necessary inferences (1362[a]21–34). Similarly in the second book Aristotle introduces a definition of anger beginning with 'let-it-be' and then goes on to draw certain inferences whose logical relationship to the definition is emphasised by the formula 'if this is anger, then it is necessary' (1378[a]30–3; cf. 1382[a]21–8). In other words Aristotle's treatment of emotions, like his earlier treatment of particular premises, shows us how Aristotle brought a deductive method to rhetorical study and so helped meet the demand for a philosophical rhetoric.[3]

[1] Since these two books of the *Rhetoric* (with the exception of certain later additions like 2.23–4) belong to the period of Aristotle's residence in Plato's Academy (see, for example, I. Düring, *Aristoteles* [Heidelberg 1966] 118–21), they can be viewed as a contribution to the study of rhetoric in the Academy.

[2] On *estô* or 'let-it-be' as part of the vocabulary of demonstration see my 'Aristotle's Rhetoric on Emotions', *Archiv für Geschichte der Philosophie* 52 (1970) 45–53.

[3] Aristotle's deductive method agrees formally with the procedure recommended by Plato in the *Phaedrus*. A *logos* should begin with a definition (263[d]2–3) and subsequent portions should be arranged according to a certain necessity (*anagkê*, 264[b]4, 7). Still this portion of the *Phaedrus* is not Aristotle's

Of even greater significance for rhetoric is the fact that Aristotle's analysis of emotion made clear the relationship of emotion to reasoned argumentation. By construing thought or belief as the efficient cause of emotion, Aristotle showed that emotional response is intelligent behaviour open to reasoned persuasion. When men are angered, they are not victims of some totally irrational force. Rather they are responding in accordance with the thought of unjust insult. Their belief may be erroneous and their anger unreasonable, but their behaviour is intelligent and cognitive in the sense that it is grounded upon a belief which may be criticised and even altered by argumentation. Of course, this was long recognised in practice. We may mention again how Pericles summoned an assembly and tried by speaking to affect the emotions of the Athenian people (Thuc. 2.65.1). He was only partially successful. He was able to persuade the Athenians to prosecute the war with greater zeal (2.65.2), but he failed to remove completely their anger and was fined by them. Still, Pericles' attempt to alter the anger of Athenian citizens was not foolish. Perhaps quite unconsciously he understood that anger is grounded upon and directed by beliefs which can be changed by reasoned argument. But practice is not always theory, and it is a point of some interest that professional rhetoricians like Thrasymachus and Gorgias spoke of emotional appeals as charms and enchantments (Plato, *Phdr.* 267^{c}7–^{d}1, Gorg., *Hel.* 10, 14). Neither rhetorician seems to have investigated the nature of emotional response and in the absence of such an investigation it was easy to think of emotions as diseases whose victims suffer a misfortune (*Hel.* 19) curable only by drugs and inspired incantations (*Hel.* 10, 14).

As long as this view of emotional response and emotional appeal remained uncorrected, emotional appeal could be conceived of as

---

primary inspiration. For here Plato is concerned fundamentally with the organic unity of a *logos* (264^{c}2–5) and possibly with the method of division (265^{d}3–266^{b}1) which he calls dialectic (266^{e}1, *Phil.* 17^{a}4). In employing a deductive method to analyse emotional response Aristotle seems to be guided primarily by his own *Analytics* which seem to have been written either concurrently with or just before the second book of the *Rhetoric*. (See Düring, *Aristoteles*, 119 with note 7, and F. Solmsen, *Die Entwicklung der aristotelischen Logik und Rhetorik* [Berlin 1929] 223.) In his use of *estô* Aristotle seems to be drawing on the vocabulary of the *Analytics* (e.g., *An. Post.* 75^{b}6, 9; 81^{b}30; 94^{b}14; 98^{b}26; 99^{a}31) and in defining the individual emotions he seems to be offering causal definitions that meet the standards of the *Posterior Analytics* (see above, Section 2).

something suspect and altogether different from reasoned argumentation. We can understand why Gorgias made Palamedes tell the jury of Greek leaders that he would not try to arouse their pity but rather would try to instruct them in truth (*Pal.* 33). Similarly we can understand why Plato made Socrates reject emotional appeal in favour of instruction (*Apol.* 35^{b}9–^{c}2). Viewed as an affliction divorced from cognition, emotion was naturally opposed to reason and conceived of as something hostile to thoughtful judgment. It was Aristotle's contribution to offer a very different view of emotion, so that emotional appeal would no longer be viewed as an extra-rational enchantment. Once Aristotle focused on the cognitive side of emotional response and made clear that an emotion can be altered by argument because beliefs can be altered in this way, it was possible to adopt a positive attitude towards emotional appeal. There was no need to confine emotional appeals to prooemium and epilogue, for emotions can and should be aroused and allayed throughout an oration by reasoned argumentation. Expressed in Aristotelian terminology, persuasion 'through the hearers' could be recognised as an effective means of persuasion and also elevated to a position coordinate with persuasion 'through demonstration'.

4. *A contribution to poetics*

The consequences for poetics were similar to those for rhetoric. Mimetic or imitative poetry and in particular tragedy and comedy were related to cognitive emotions and therefore recognised as art forms evoking intelligent responses compatible with reason. This is a point of some importance, for in the *Republic* Plato had set up an opposition between reason and emotion (604^{a}10–^{b}4), and had severely criticised the writers of tragedy and comedy for playing upon feelings that are unintelligent (605^{b}8) and destructive of man's reasoning capacity (605^{b}4–5). He had associated dramatic poetry with what is most irrational (604^{d}9) and had challenged her fans to show that in addition to providing pleasure poetry offers some benefit to human society and life (607^{d}8–9). The Academic investigation of emotion was a fundamental step toward meeting these criticisms. Once emotional responses were seen to be complex phenomena involving thoughts as well as physiological changes, Aristotle was able not only to associate tragedy with fear (*phobos*) and pity (*eleos*) and comedy with the laughable or ridiculous (*geloion*) but also to develop a theory of benefit through purgation (*katharsis*).

The association of tragedy with fear and pity was not altogether original with Aristotle (*Poet.* 1449^{a}27, 1452^{b}32–3). Gorgias had spoken of fearful shuddering and tearful pity and grievous longing entering persons listening to poetry and then had gone on to mention enchantments which charm the soul (*Hel.* 9–10). The importance here is not the connection of poetry with two emotions subsequently picked out by Aristotle as peculiarly tragic emotions. Rather it is the connection with charms and enchantments. Poetry, like rhetoric, was compared with extra-rational phenomena that work upon emotions in the way that drugs work upon the body (cf. *Hel.* 14). Against this background we can understand Plato's charges against dramatic poetry. Grouped together with charms and drugs dramatic poetry could be thought of as an enchantment that played upon feelings which are unintelligent and irrational (*Rep.* 604^{d}9, 605^{b}8). But later when fear was shown to be not simply a shuddering but also and essentially an expectation of destructive or painful evil (*Rhet.* 1382^{a}21–2, ^{b}29–34) and when pity was referred not only to the thought of unmerited suffering but also to educated men who reason well (1385^{b}13–16, 27), Plato's charges against tragic poetry lost their force. Tragedy was associated with two emotions which were recognised not only as intelligent and reasonable responses but also as important controls in determining the kinds of actions depicted in tragic poetry. Plato had criticised poets for representing unjust men as happy and just men as wretched (*Rep.* 392^{a}13–^{b}2).[1] Aristotle did not reverse this criticism, but he was able to substitute a peculiarly poetic explanation for Plato's moral structure. Having tied tragedy to pity and fear, he was able to show that a tragic plot, or at least a well-constructed plot, cannot represent the good man suffering misfortune nor the vicious man experiencing good fortune, for in neither case are the tragic emotions of pity and fear aroused. A virtuous man moving from good to bad fortune is, according to Aristotle, neither fearful nor pitiable but rather shocking or revolting and a vicious man changing from bad to good fortune appeals neither to ordinary human sympathy nor to pity and fear (1452^{b}34–1453^{a}1). In other words, the very plots that Plato had thought dangerous to impressionable minds and therefore

---

[1] Cf. G. Else, *Aristotle's Poetics: the Argument* (Cambridge 1963) 373–4.

reprehensible on moral and educational grounds were shown by Aristotle to be deficient in regard to the peculiarly tragic emotions and therefore to be undesirable on purely poetic grounds. That constituted a significant advance in dramatic criticism.

The association of comedy with the laughable or ridiculous was also of especial importance for poetic theory. In the *Republic*, Plato had criticised not only tragedy but also comedy for helping to erode the control of reason (606ᶜ2–9, cf. 388ᵉ5–389ᵇ1), and in the *Philebus* he had connected comedy with the emotion of envy (*phthonos*) and with the pleasure envious men take in the ills and mistakes of their neighbours (48ᵃ8–50ᵇ6). Aristotle did not undo the entire Platonic analysis. He accepted the connection with mistakes (*Poet.* 1449ᵃ34–5, cf. *Phil.* 48ᵉ9) and the general idea that laughter is an emotional response. But he dropped the connection with envy, and moved away from the tragi-comedy of life (*Phil.* 50ᵇ3) to the purely dramatic comedy of the stage. He restricted the laughable or ridiculous to mistakes and deformities that are neither painful nor destructive (1449ᵃ34–5)[1] and moved towards a notion of laughter which could not be tied to bad moral character in the way that envy could be tied to injustice (*Phil.* 49ᵈ7, cf. *Rhet.* 1386ᵇ33–7ᵃ3) and which could become the basis of a superiority theory of humour. Aristotle's detailed remarks on comedy are lost with the second book of the *Poetics*, but his brief remarks in the first book of the *Poetics* together with scattered notices in the *Rhetoric* suggest strongly that Aristotle's own investigation of emotional response had led him to a position not unlike that of Hobbes, who defined the passion of laughter as 'sudden glory arising from some sudden conception of some eminency in ourselves by comparison with the inferiority of others, or with our own formerly'.[2] For Aristotle wittiness is educated insolence and

---

[1] While the idea of mistakes that are neither painful nor destructive has a clear antecedent in Plato's *Philebus* (the ignorance appropriate to comedy is said to be weak and harmless [49ᵃ7–ᶜ5, ᵉ2–4]), the mention of ugly deformity seems to involve a departure from and even an improvement upon the *Philebus*. For in this Platonic dialogue ugliness is introduced only in connection with false opinions concerning personal appearance (48ᵉ4–6, 49ᵈ11). Such a connection may be common, but it does not seem necessary for comic humour. Aristotle quite correctly points to comic masks (1449ᵃ36) which are not only distorted but also funny quite apart from any erroneous beliefs concerning personal appearance.

[2] *Human Nature* in W. Molesworth (ed.), *The English Works of Thomas Hobbes* (London 1840) 4.46.

insolence involves being pleased by the thought of one's own superiority (*Rhet.* 1389^{b}11–12, 1378^{b}23–8). The idea of *educated* insolence is important. Aristotle does not endorse unqualified delight in superiority. Crude insolence is a mark of poor education and something to be avoided.[1] Similarly on the comic stage personal abuse or invective (*psogos*) is primitive and less desirable than the laughable or ridiculous (1448^{b}25–9^{a}2). Much as Aristotle's analysis of pity and fear had led him to restrict the kinds of plots that are suitable to tragedy, so his interest in the laughable seems to have helped him develop a refined notion of comedy. He came to see that the emotional response appropriate to comedy is neither the laughter of an envious man nor the laughter which follows upon personal abuse. Rather it is the laughter that follows upon perceiving mistakes and deformities which do not cause pain or destruction and only those plays which present such mistakes and deformities are satisfactory comedies capable of evoking the comic emotion of finding something funny.

Finally, it should be recalled that Aristotle adopted an inclusive view of emotional response. He recognised both its cognitive and its bodily aspects. This meant that Aristotle could not only reject the Platonic suggestion that dramatic poetry plays to unintelligent feelings divorced from reason but also meet the Platonic demand for a positive benefit to human life (*Rep.* 607^{d}8–9). He was able to develop a theory of purgation which in the *Poetics* is associated with tragedy (1449^{b}27–8) and in the *Politics* with enthusiastic music (1341^{b}32–2^{a}15). Aristotle's theory of purgation is, of course, a much debated doctrine whose connection with comedy is at best speculative.[2] But without taking on all the issues involved in the scholarly debate we can say that the idea of tragedy purging or purifying pity and fear compliments the idea of tragedy appealing to intelligent emotions and shows how right Aristotle was to favour an inclusive analysis of emotional response. Fear, for example, is never simply a matter of unpleasant sensations. It involves certain thoughts which within the sphere of poetics help to determine what sorts of plots are

---

[1] See my 'Aristotle and the Questionable Mean-Dispositions', *Transactions of the American Philological Association* 99 (1968) 216–19.

[2] The connection with comedy is explicit in the Peripatetic *Tractatus Coislinianus*. For an introduction to the problems concerning comic purgation see Lane Cooper, *An Aristotelian Theory of Comedy* (New York 1922) 5–6, 60–98, 224.

appropriate to tragedy. But similarly fear is never simply a matter of having certain thoughts. It also involves the body (*De An.* 403ᵃ16-19) and in particular a change in bodily temperature. Even in the *Rhetoric* where Aristotle emphasises that being frightened involves an expectation of suffering (1382ᵇ29-34) he recognises the connection of fear with bodily condition and states that old age involves a drop in temperature which prepares the way for cowardice (1389ᵇ29-32). In the *Parts of Animals* the disposition of timorous creatures is explained by watery blood (650ᵇ27-30) and in the *Problems* a disposition to be frightened is connected with cold black bile (954ᵇ4-14). This portion of the *Problems* may be Theophrastean, but the idea was probably accepted by Aristotle and in any event Aristotle's general commitment to physiological explanation is clear enough. Perhaps we can say that Aristotle understood the way in which emotional response varies according to bodily condition and used this understanding to develop a homoeopathic theory of purgation.[1] In watching and responding to a tragedy the spectator is not only stimulated intellectually. He is also purged in so far as his bodily condition is altered. He undergoes a quasi-medical treatment (cf. *Pol.* 1342ᵃ10) which improves his disposition in regard to the everyday emotions of fear and pity.

[1] See D. W. Lucas, *Aristotle; Poetics* (Oxford 1968) 283.

CHAPTER TWO

A New Political-Ethical Psychology

1. *The development of a bipartite psychology*

The Academic investigation of emotion was to have its greatest consequences in the fields of politics and ethics. Once emotions were focused upon and recognised as a special class of cognitive phenomena open to reasoned persuasion in a way that bodily drives are not, it was possible to develop a peculiarly human psychology which could replace Plato's tripartite psychology. We can see this psychology being developed in Plato's *Laws* and then fully formulated in Aristotle's *Politics* and *Ethics*. Much as Plato's *Philebus* seems to be raising questions about emotions that are answered by Aristotle in the *Rhetoric*, so the *Laws* seems to be working towards a psychology that Aristotle ultimately made his own and exploited within his political and ethical writings. The soul came to be divided into alogical and logical halves and all emotions came to be collected together within the alogical half. The relationship of emotion to reasoned argumentation was recognised in the obedience of the alogical half to the logical half and the distinction between moral virtue and practical wisdom was made to coincide with this new psychic dichotomy.

Concerning the *Laws* there is little need to argue that Plato works primarily with an implicit or unformulated bipartite psychology. This is almost a commonplace among scholars today.[1] What needs to be emphasised is that this dichotomy presupposes the Academic investigation of emotion and cannot be construed intelligibly as a

[1] See, for example, H. Görgemanns, *Beiträge zur Interpretation von Platons Nomoi* (München 1960) 122, 137, 142; D. Rees, 'Bipartition of the Soul in the Early Academy', *Journal of Hellenic Studies* 77 (1957) 115–16; A. Graeser, *Probleme der platonischen Seelenteilungslehre* (München 1969) 100–105; T. Robinson, *Plato's Psychology* (Toronto 1970) 145. Even T. Saunders ('The Structure of the Soul and the State in Plato's Laws', *Eranos* 60 [1962] 37–55) who argues for a tripartite soul in the *Laws* does not deny the appearance of dichotomy. His claim is that 'the bipartite analysis can never *exclude* the tripartite' (37, cf. 42).

23

distinction between sensations and impulses on the one hand and all kinds of cognition on the other. In the *Laws* it is quite clear that emotions are conceived of as cognitive phenomena distinct from and yet related to the reasonings of *logismos*. We may refer to the first book where the Athenian Stranger undertakes a brief discussion of human motivation. The discussion begins with the statement that each of us is one (644^{c}4) and then proceeds to consider in three steps factors which determine human behaviour. First, pleasure (*hêdonê*) and pain (*lupê*) are named and called opposed and foolish counsellors (644^{c}6–7). Then expectation (*elpis*) is mentioned and divided into fear (*phobos*) in the face of pain and confidence (*tharros*) before the opposite (644^{c}9–^{d}1). Finally calculation (*logismos*) is introduced and related to law (644^{d}1–3). Since this list is hardly more than a bare enumeration, a puppet image is introduced to elucidate its meaning. According to this image each individual is a puppet whose actions are determined by cords of which one is described as the soft, golden cord of calculation (645^{a}1, 3) and contrasted with other cords that are hard and iron (645^{a}2–3). This makes clear that what had seemed to be a threefold division is to be construed primarily as a dichotomy. Pleasure and pain and fear and confidence are grouped together as iron cords in contrast with the golden cord of calculation.

We have, it seems, a dichotomy. But how are we to construe this dichotomy? One way already suggested in the literature is to explain pleasure and pain, confidence and fear as impulses and to oppose these impulses to thought.[1] This way we get a dichotomy between thrusts and cognition—all judgment and opinion being assigned to the latter member of the dichotomy.[2] Such an interpretation is unsatisfactory. For fear and confidence are introduced explicitly as *doxai* or opinions and *elpis* or expectation is declared a common name for opinions concerning the future (644^{c}9–^{d}1).[3]

[1] Görgemanns, *Beiträge* 119–29, cf. 137–42.

[2] Görgemanns (*Beiträge* 120, 122, cf. 127, 137, 155) opposes 'Triebe' to 'Einsicht' or more generally 'eine geistige Kraft'. Cf. Graeser (*Probleme* 101) who says that the ethical views of the *Laws* are oriented towards a 'Dualismus zwischen Einsicht und Trieben'.

[3] The common or generic usage of *elpis* and its cognate forms is illustrated clearly at *Philebus* 32^{b}9–^{c}2 where Socrates introduces the idea of a pleasant or painful expectation (*prosdokêma*) that belongs to the soul itself. The influence of the *Philebus*, direct and indirect, upon the *Laws* and the development of a new political-ethical psychology is hard to overstate.

Instead of identifying fear, confidence and other emotions with non-cognitive thrusts, the Athenian Stranger recognises the involvement of thought in emotional response and accordingly sets up a dichotomy between two different kinds of cognitive activity—namely, emotional response and reasoned reflection. This does not mean that the *Laws* refuses altogether to speak of emotions as, say, disturbances (*tarachai* 632ᵃ3). Emotions are disturbing in that they regularly involve some sort of bodily sensation and often upset a man's ability to reason well and judge correctly. But emotions are not simply disturbances. They are in part at least cognitive phenomena and (as the *Philebus* had already made clear) are to be distinguished from bodily sensations like itches and tickles and bodily drives like hunger and thirst. After considerable discussion members of the Academy were quite clear that emotions like fear and confidence are grounded upon opinions or assessments. The Athenian Stranger is no exception, and as the dialogue progresses he reaffirms the involvement of cognition in fear (646ᵉ7–8, 647ᵉ3) and confidence (649ᵇ2–3). Furthermore, when the Athenian Stranger speaks of *logismos* considering the relative merits of emotions like fear and confidence (644ᵈ2), he is thinking neither of measuring the intensity of certain thrusts and drives nor of comparing pleasant and painful sensations. Rather he is concerned with reflecting upon and valuing different ways of responding to a given situation: e.g., reflecting upon the emotion of shame and its merits in comparison with shameless confidence (646ᵉ10–647ᵇ1). This is not to say that the reflections of *logismos* never concern pleasant and painful sensations. Nor is it to say that the *Laws* makes no room for pleasant and painful sensations. It is only to say that pleasant and painful sensations, thrusts and drives are not the whole story or even the most important part of it. The reflections of an individual (644ᶜ4) moral agent, like those of students of law (636ᵈ5), are concerned primarily with pleasant and painful emotional responses. The dichotomy implicit in the *Laws* is fundamentally a distinction between calculations and reflections on the one hand and pleasant and painful emotions such as fear and confidence on the other. It presupposes work done in the *Philebus* and looks forward to Aristotle's political and ethical writings and to a fully formulated dichotomy between alogical and logical halves of the soul (*Pol.* 1333ᵃ17, 1334ᵇ18–19; *EN* 1102ᵇ13–1103ᵃ3, 1139ᵃ3–5).

2. *A peculiarly human psychology*

Aristotle's alogical-logical distinction is a formulation of the bipartite psychology latent in Plato's *Laws*. It marks off emotional response from reasoned deliberation, locates all emotion within the alogical half and asserts a relation of obedience between psychic halves. In other words, it recognises that emotions are cognitive phenomena open to reason and builds this recognition into a psychological framework well suited for drawing distinctions between modes of cognitive and therefore human behaviour. This is a point of some importance, for scholars have tended to confuse Aristotle's political and ethical psychology with his biological psychology familiar to readers of the *De Anima*. They have tended to assume that the biological distinction between sensation and cognition corresponds to the political and ethical distinction between alogical and logical halves of the soul.[1] This is unfortunate, for Aristotle does not confuse politics and ethics with biological investigation. In doing politics and ethics he is concerned with human beings and accordingly makes use of a psychological framework that focuses on different kinds of cognitive behaviour. In doing biology Aristotle is concerned with a broader spectrum of living things. He is interested in plants and animals as well as human beings and therefore adopts a biological psychology that corresponds

[1] The history of this confusion may be traced back to R. Loening (*Die Zurechnungslehre des Aristoteles* [Jena 1903]) who thought that the biological distinction between *nous* and *orexis* could be identified with the ethical distinction between practical wisdom and moral virtue (38) and twice began an account of *die praktische Vernunft* by considering passages in the *De Anima* (18, 28). D. Allan ('Aristotle's Account of the Origin of Moral Principles', *Proceedings of the Eleventh International Congress of Philosophy* 12 [1953] 122–3) approved of Loening's use of the biological psychology to elucidate ethical distinctions and in his own work (*The Philosophy of Aristotle* [London 1952] 75–8, 180–2) advanced a similar thesis. J. Walsh (*Aristotle's Conception of Moral Weakness* [New York 1963] 132, cf. 83) and J. Monan (*Moral Knowledge and its Methodology in Aristotle* [Oxford 1968] 50) have approved of Allan's use of the biological psychology and T. Ando (*Aristotle's Theory of Practical Cognition* [Sakyo 1958] 91–2, 99–101, 137–8) has tacitly followed Loening in relating the bipartite and biological psychologies. See also J. Burnet (*The Ethics of Aristotle* [London 1900] 63–5) who relates the biological faculties of sensation and motive force to the alogical half of the bipartite soul and W. Hardy (*Aristotle's Ethical Theory* [Oxford 1968] 70, 73) who does not accept a radical difference between the ethical and biological psychologies and argues for broad agreement between the *Ethics* and *De Anima* in regard to the soul.

to the differences between plant, animal and human life. He works with a threefold distinction between nutritive, sensitive and cognitive faculties and not with a twofold distinction between emotion and reason.[1]

Here a caveat is in order. I do not want to suggest that Aristotle never makes use of his biological psychology in political and ethical investigation. On occasion he certainly does introduce his biological framework to help make a particular point. An instructive case occurs in the first book of the *Nicomachean Ethics* where Aristotle makes use of the biological psychology in an effort to pin down the function peculiar to mankind. A simple nutritive life is rejected on the grounds that such a life is shared by plants and therefore not peculiar to man. Similarly a sensitive life is ruled out as common to horse, ox and all animals. This rejection leaves the life of intelligence which Aristotle describes as an active life of that which possesses *logos*. Clearly Aristotle is using his biological psychology and with good reason. At this moment he is thinking of men in relation to plants and animals and therefore adopts an appropriate framework. But for the most part Aristotle's political and ethical investigations concern distinctions within the sphere of human activity, so that an exclusively human framework is in order. Moreover, even when Aristotle considers the function peculiar to men and thinks of men in relation to plants and animals, he does not entirely forget his political and ethical dichotomy. Rather he adds a kind of footnote which relates the political and ethical psychology to the biological psychology by locating both the alogical and logical halves of the soul within the biological faculty of intelligence ($1097^b33-1098^a5$). Aristotle may be prompted to add this note because his mode of

---

[1] D. W. Hamlyn (*Aristotle's De Anima* [Oxford 1968] xii–xiii) complains that the *De Anima* does not offer a satisfactory treatment of emotional response and that for Aristotle's account of emotion we must turn to the second book of the *Rhetoric*. In fairness to Aristotle two points should be made. First, there is nothing very wrong with turning to other works, and had it survived Aristotle's *Diaireseis* may have contained an additional and perhaps even more fundamental account of emotion than that which survives in the *Rhetoric* (see below, p. 29 n.1). Secondly, part of the reason why the *De Anima* generally ignores emotion seems to be that emotion cannot be assigned to a particular faculty of the biological psychology. Fear, for example, is a complex phenomenon involving the thought of impending danger, unpleasant feelings and a desire for safety. It therefore brings into play several biological faculties (*nous, aisthêsis, orexis*) and lacks a single *locus* within Aristotle's biological framework.

introducing the biological faculty of intelligence invites confusion with the logical half of bipartition.[1] Alternatively he may simply think it prudent after using the biological psychology to add a note relating this psychology to the bipartite psychology fundamental to political and ethical discussion. Whatever Aristotle's reason for adding this note, it is significant in "that it rules out identifying the logical half of bipartition with the biological faculty of intelligence and the alogical half with the biological faculty of sensation.

Of equal interest are Aristotle's remarks at the end of the first book of the *Ethics*. Here Aristotle refers to Cretan and Spartan legislators (1102ᵃ10–11), tells us that the man who is truly concerned with politics wishes to make citizens good (1102ᵃ9) and emphasises the need to study human virtue (1102ᵃ14). We are reminded of the *Laws* which not only focuses on the legislators of Crete and Sparta but also directs lawgivers to have as their aim that men become good and possess the virtue of soul appropriate to mankind (770ᶜ5–ᵈ2). These points of agreement with the *Laws* are not surprising in a chapter that introduces the dichotomy implicit in the *Laws*, now formulated in terms of logical and alogical halves of

---

[1] The phrase 'that which possesses *logos*' is used commonly to refer to the logical half of the bipartite soul (1102ᵃ28, 1139ᵃ4, *Pol.* 1333ᵃ17), but here at 1098ᵃ3–4 it is used to refer to the biological faculty of intelligence. There is nothing wrong with this latter usage, which becomes clear if we follow R. Hicks (Aristotle, *De Anima* [Cambridge 1907] 456) and compare this portion of the *Ethics* with *De Anima* 427ᵇ8–14 where Aristotle distinguishes thinking from sensing partly on the grounds that sensing belongs to all animals, while thinking is found only where *logos* is found. In other words, *logos* is considered a distinguishing mark of intelligence and human beings (cf. 428ᵃ23–4). Accordingly in the *Ethics* when Aristotle is thinking in terms of his biological psychology, he introduces *logos* as a distinguishing mark of intelligence. Since this usage of *logos* is potentially confusing in an ethical treatise whose primary psychic framework distinguishes between logical and alogical halves, it may be that Aristotle adds a note explaining the relationship of the biological faculty of intelligence to the logical and alogical halves of the bipartite soul. For the sake of completeness it should be mentioned that *zôiou* could be understood with *tou logon echontos* (1098ᵃ3–4) and *logon* could be taken as the antecedent of *toutou* (1098ᵃ4). This way of construing the passage avoids no difficulties and seems to me less plausible, so that I am inclined to follow, e.g., R. Gauthier and J. Jolif (*L'Éthique à Nicomaque* [Louvain 1959] 1.15), F. Dirlmeier (*Aristoteles, Nikomachische Ethik* [Berlin 1960] 14) and M. Ostwald (*Aristotle, Nicomachean Ethics*, Library of Liberal Arts edition [Indianapolis 1962] 16) in taking *tou logon echontos* as the antecedent of *toutou*.

the soul (1102ᵃ28).[1] As we have seen in the preceding section, the *Laws* works with a basic distinction between reasoning and emotional response and looks upon emotion as a cognitive phenomenon open to reasoned persuasion. The *Ethics* is working within a similar framework, when it emphasises persuading the alogical half through reasoned admonition and considers saying that the alogical half

[1] At *EN* 1102ᵃ26–7, Aristotle says that he has discussed the soul in the *exôterikoi logoi* and that these *logoi* should be made use of. The identity of the *exôterikoi logoi* has been a topic of scholarly debate too voluminous to survey in this place. Perhaps I may simply assert my own view that Aristotle is referring either to his *Theses Concerning the Soul* (D.L. 5.24) or more probably to his *Diaireseis* which seems to have touched upon tripartition (fr. 3 Ross) and therefore may have marked off the dichotomy of political-ethical investigation from tripartition and other psychic frameworks. This view is, of course, speculative, but it receives some support from the fact that when Aristotle considers the ideal constitution and tells us that much has been said about the best life in the *exôterikoi logoi*, he introduces straightway a generally accepted *diairesis* of goods into external, bodily and psychic goods (*Pol.* 1323ᵃ24–7). The use of the term *diairesis* in close conjunction with the phrase *exôterikoi logoi* may or may not be significant, but it seems more than likely that the classification of goods was discussed in the *Diaireseis* and that Aristotle's remarks concerning the best life draw directly or indirectly on that discussion. Similarly when Aristotle treats emotions and tells us that it is necessary to divide or analyse (*diairein*, *Rhet.* 1378ᵃ22) each emotion in three respects, he may be drawing on a previous discussion in the *Diaireseis*. And finally when Aristotle divides the logical half of the bipartite soul into practical and theoretical portions and observes that he is dividing (*diairein*) in his accustomed manner (*Pol.* 1333ᵃ24–5), he may be thinking of his *Diaireseis*. This is, to be sure, no more than a guess, but it seems to be a reasonable one and to fit well with developments in Plato's Academy. We have observed already that when Plato wrote the *Philebus* emotion was under investigation within the Academy, and that when Aristotle wrote the *Topics* there was already a preference for explaining the cognition involved in emotion as the efficient cause mentioned in the essential definition. The *Diaireseis* may have recorded the results of this investigation, including not only an analysis of emotions but also a new political-ethical psychology. For a better understanding of emotional responses as cognitive phenomena led naturally enough to a new psychology which collected together emotions within a single psychic half that is itself cognitive and therefore open to the persuasion of reasoned reflections. Whether both steps—the analysis of emotional response and the formulation of a new psychic dichotomy based upon this analysis—were recorded in the *Diaireseis* cannot be proven with certainty. But it seems a reasonable conjecture to say that the *Diaireseis* discussed bipartition and marked off this new political-ethical psychology from other psychological frameworks like tripartition. And if this conjecture is reasonable, then it may also be reasonable to suggest that when the *Ethics* refers to the *exôterikoi logoi* for an adequate discussion of bipartition, the reference is to Aristotle's own *Diaireseis*.

possesses *logos* (1102ᵇ31–1103ᵃ3). Emotion, that is to say the alogical behaviour of human beings, involves judgment and therefore is open to reasoned persuasion and properly classified among cognitive phenomena.[1] The only complication in the *Ethics* passage is that Aristotle divides the alogical half of the soul and associates one portion with the biological faculty of nutrition (1102ᵃ32–ᵇ12). As earlier in the discussion of man's function, the introduction of the biological psychology is potentially confusing. The obedient portion of the alogical soul might be confused with the biological faculty of sensation and the logical half of the soul with the biological faculty of intelligence. To guard against this confusion Aristotle adds a note stating that the obedient portion of the soul might be said to possess *logos*. This brief note recalls the earlier note at 1098ᵃ4–5 and effectively prevents confusing this obedient portion with the biological faculty of sensation.[2] For this biological faculty is not a cognitive faculty and cannot be said plausibly to possess *logos*. In contrast, the alogical nature characteristic of children is cognitive, is attentive to the reasoned admonitions of a father (1102ᵇ32, 1103ᵃ3) and can be associated plausibly with *logos*. It is part of a human psychology whose development presupposes the Academic investigation of emotion. First the cognitive nature of emotion was analysed and then a new political and ethical psychology was developed. The relation of emotion to reason was formulated in terms of alogical and logical psychic halves.[3]

---

[1] Aristotle is quite clear concerning the futility of using persuasion to stop a man from feeling hot or hungry (1113ᵃ26–30). Such feelings have bodily causes and differ from emotions which are grounded upon judgments and so open to persuasion by the logical half of the bipartite soul.

[2] A connection between 1098ᵃ4–5 and 1103ᵃ1–3 has long been recognised and often commented upon. See J. Bernays, *Die Dialoge des Aristoteles* [Berlin 1863] 157–8; Loening, *Zurechnungslehre* 91–2, note 17; Dirlmeier, *Nikomachische* 292–3, Gauthier and Jolif, *L'Éthique* 2.57. 98, and my 'Zu der Darstellung der Seele in der Nikomachischen Ethik I 13', *Philologus* 114 (1970) 289–91.

[3] The preceding remarks have drawn upon statements in the *Nicomachean Ethics*. It may be added that the *Eudemian Ethics* is equally clear concerning its interest in a peculiarly human psychology. Since we are investigating human virtue, the *Eudemian Ethics* states, let it be assumed that the soul has two parts, each of which possesses *logos*, though not in the same way. One part possesses *logos* in that it naturally gives orders and the other part possesses *logos* in that it naturally obeys and listens (1219ᵇ27–31). This emphasis upon human virtue agrees with the *Nicomachean Ethics* (1102ᵃ14, 16, ᵇ3, 12) as does the idea of possessing *logos* in the sense of obeying and listening (1102ᵇ31, 1103ᵃ3). For us

3. An advance over tripartition as a political-ethical psychology

The psychic dichotomy implicit in the *Laws* and fully formulated in Aristotle's *Politics* and *Ethics* is a new development and a significant advance over tripartition as employed by Plato in the *Republic*. This is an important point, for certain scholars have tended to assume that Aristotle's political and ethical dichotomy was always latent in tripartition and that the Aristotelian distinction between alogical and logical halves of the soul arose out of tripartition by simply assigning the spirited part of the soul (*thymoeides*) to the appetitive part (*epithymētikon*) so as to form a simple alogical half (cf. Plut., *Mor.* 442B). The spirited part, it has been suggested, was always in an ambiguous position between the reasoning or calculating part (*logistikon*) and the appetitive part. Its independent status was tied up with the threefold structure of Plato's ideal state, so that whenever this political framework receded into the background, the spirited part could be conceived of in terms of an emotion like anger and joined to the appetitive part to form the alogical or emotional side of man.[1] A decisive reason for rejecting this idea is that

[1] See F. M. Cornford, 'Psychology and Social Structure in the Republic of Plato', *Classical Quarterly* 6 (1912) 246–65; R. Hackforth, 'The Modification of Plan in Plato's Republic', *Classical Quarterly* 7 (1913) 265–72; Rees, 'Bipartition' 114; Robinson, *Psychology* 39, 44, 120; T. Penner, 'Thought and Desire in Plato' in G. Vlastos (ed.), *Plato II* (Garden City 1971) 113.

the important point is that the *Eudemian Ethics* not only connects bipartition with human virtue but also insists that the two parts of the bipartite soul are peculiar to the human soul (1219^{b}37–8). The reason why both parts are said to be peculiar to the human soul is that both parts are cognitive. We may compare how the *Nichomachean Ethics* locates the division of bipartition within the biological faculty of intelligence (1098^{a}4–5) and thereby indicates that both halves are cognitive and peculiar to human beings. The *Eudemian Ethics* is saying the same thing, only it goes on to state that the excellences of the nutritive and motive faculties are not the special property of man (1219^{b}38–9). Animals possess the biological faculty of motive force in conjunction with sensation. But these faculties alone are not sufficient for action. The *Nicomachean Ethics* recognises this (1139^{a}20) and so does the *Eudemian Ethics* in that it makes action a mark of human beings (1219^{b}40, 1222^{b}19). Bipartition as a moral psychology is concerned primarily with two modes of human action. Its fundamental division is not between intelligence and sensation together with motive force but rather between reasoning and emotional response (1220^{a}1–2). Both reasoning and emotional response are cognitive and therefore human activities. With this in mind the *Eudemian Ethics* says that both halves of the bipartite soul are peculiar to human beings.

Aristotle locates not only spirit (*thymos*) and appetite (*epithymia*) but also wish (*boulêsis*) within the alogical half of the bipartite soul (*Pol.* 1334ᵇ22–3). In other words, Aristotle draws on the Academic investigation of emotion, collects together all desire and emotion and contrasts this group of psychic phenomena with deliberation, reflection and in general calculation (*logismos*). To be sure, the *Republic* does conceive of the reasoning part of the soul as that part which calculates (*logizesthai*: 439ᵈ5, cf. 441ᶜ1). But it does not restrict the reasoning part to ratiocination or more generally to intellectual activity and makes no attempt to collect together all emotion and desire within the lower two psychic parts. In fact the *Republic* is quite explicit that each of the three psychic parts has its own desires. To the appetitive part are referred hunger, thirst, sexual appetite, and a desire for money and gain. The spirited part is connected with a desire for dominance and honour, while the reasoning part is connected with a desire for knowledge and therefore labelled 'lover of learning' and 'lover of wisdom' (580ᵈ7–1ᵇ10). The reasoning part is even said to wish to follow calculation (604ᵈ5–6) and to manifest itself as a psychic impulse or drive at moments of inner conflict (604ᵇ3–4). Furthermore, shame, an emotion of considerable importance in regard to human conduct, is associated with the reasoning part (571ᶜ9, 606ᵉ3–6; cf. Ar., *Topics* 126ᵃ8). This contrasts with the *Laws* where shame is treated together with fear (646ᵉ4–647ᵃ2) and shameless confidence (647ᵃ10), neither of which can be plausibly connected with the reasoning part of tripartition. When Plato wrote the *Republic*, he and other members of the Academy had not yet focused upon emotional response and therefore were not alert to the possibility of grouping together emotions and forming a new political and ethical psychology that opposed emotional response to reasoned reflection. But when Plato wrote the *Laws*, he and other members of the Academy had focused on emotion and were beginning to formulate a new psychology that grouped shame and other emotions together within one psychic half.[1]

---

[1] There are, of course, difficulties in locating shame within any one particular psychic part. The connection of shamelessness with courage (561ᵃ1) and of feeling ashamed with being frightened (562ᵉ8–9) may suggest locating shame as well as fear within the spirited part. The *Phaedrus* connects shame with the so-called good horse (253ᵈ6, 254ᵃ2, ᵉ4, 256ᵃ6) and therefore seems to refer this emotion to the spirited part. Nevertheless, these passages should not be used to

A further reason for refusing to see a clear anticipation of Aristotle's bipartite psychology in the *Republic* is that the two lower parts are more than casually associated with bodily drives and generally modes of behaviour appropriate to animals as well as men. In other words, the two lower parts of the tripartite soul include phenomena that are not emotions and so do not belong to the class of psychic phenomena fundamental to the alogical half of Aristotle's dichotomy. This is, of course, a matter of emphasis, for Aristotle's alogical half can be extended to include nutrition and other biological functions (*EN* 1102ᵃ32–ᵇ12). But for Aristotle such functions are not the sphere of human or moral excellence (*EN* 1102ᵇ12) and therefore are not fundamental to the dichotomy of political and ethical psychology. It is emotions like anger and fear that constitute the sphere of moral virtue and are basic to the alogical half of Aristotle's psychic dichotomy. In contrast, tripartition does not focus upon emotional responses and does not suggest that they are central to the two lower parts of the tripartite soul.

We may develop this point beginning with the appetitive part (*epithymêtikon*). This psychic part is connected with the desire for money (590ᵇ7–8) and is called on occasion the money-loving and gain-loving part of the soul (553ᶜ5, 581ᵃ6–7). Avaricious feelings are peculiarly human. They involve assessment and are properly grouped among emotional responses. But the appetitive part of the tripartite soul is not a simple faculty (580ᵈ11). It also includes bodily drives for food and drink and sexual intercourse (580ᵉ3–4). In fact such drives are fundamental to the appetitive part. In marking off the parts of the tripartite soul, Socrates calls hunger and thirst most clear cases of appetite (437ᵈ3–4) and then proceeds to use thirst as an example in establishing the existence of the appetitive part, that faculty whereby the soul feels sexual passion, hungers, thirsts and feels the flutter of other desires (439ᵈ6–8). And later when Socrates

---

reject or doubt the connection of shame with the reasoning part at *Rep.* 571ᵉ9, 606ᵉ3–6. Rather the inconsistency between passages should be construed as a sign that during this period Plato was not focusing upon emotional responses and therefore might vacillate in regard to the location of a particular emotion like shame. Concentration upon emotional responses came with the *Philebus* and resulted ultimately in collecting all emotions together within an alogical half. When Plato wrote the *Republic* this collection had not occurred. The logical part of the soul is 'not only calculative (as his term, *logistikon*, might unfortunately suggest) but passionate' (G. Vlastos, 'Justice and Psychic Harmony in the *Republic*', *The Journal of Philosophy* 66 [1969] 520).

wants to show how unreal are the pleasures of the appetitive part,
he uses hunger and thirst as examples (585ᵃ8). Hunger and thirst
and sexual drive, it seems, are central to an understanding of the
appetitive part. They are paradigm cases of appetition, but as presented in the *Republic* they do not seem to be emotional responses.
This is most obvious in regard to hunger and thirst. These two
drives are associated primarily with states of bodily depletion
(585ᵃ8–ᵇ1). Of course, Socrates recognises that hunger and thirst
may be the occasion for certain expectations (584ᶜ9; cf. *Phil.*
47ᶜ3–ᵈ3) but he does not suggest that food and drink-motivated
behaviour is in the first instance caused by particular beliefs and
assessments. The efficient cause is thought to be bodily and so very
different from the efficient cause which Aristotle makes an essential
mark of emotional response. The case of sexual desire is somewhat
less clear but the repeated association with hunger and thirst
(439ᵈ6–8, 580ᵉ3–4) and the comparison with animal behaviour
(586ᵃ7–8) suggest a non-cognitive bodily drive which is not to be
reasoned with but rather cured by age (cf. 328ᵈ2–3, 329ᵇ6–ᵈ1).[1]
This is not to say that the sexual desire of human beings cannot be
construed as a cognitive desire, and it is a point of some interest
that the *Philebus* dissociates love (*erôs*) from hunger and thirst
and groups it together with emotions belonging to the soul itself
(47ᵉ1–3). But the *Philebus* is more sophisticated than the *Republic*
in its treatment of emotions and desires and should be recognised
as a significant step on the way from tripartition to bipartition. For
our purpose the important point is that the *Republic* makes hunger,
thirst, and sexual desire fundamental to the appetitive part of the
soul and treats these desires as directed dispositions resulting from
bodily causes and therefore not open to reasoned argumentation.

---

[1] The mere fact that age brings a change in sexual desire is not for an
Aristotelian sufficient to distinguish sexual desire from emotional response.
Aristotle is quite clear that emotional response is tied to bodily condition and
therefore affected by age. Fear, for example, actually increases with age because
the body cools and so predisposes a man to this emotion (*Rhet.* 1389ᵇ31–2). Yet
fear is an emotion in the sense of a cognitive response caused by the thought of
impending danger. Sexual desire may be equally cognitive. For a discussion of
just how complex and peculiarly human sexual desire may be, see T. Nagel,
'Sexual Perversion', *The Journal of Philosophy* 66 (1969) 5–17. But sexual
activity may also be divorced from cognition. At least Aristotle recognises that
the drive to reproduce is not peculiar to men and so not peculiar to cognitive
creatures who alone are capable of emotional response (*Pol.* 1252ᵃ28–30).

Yet Aristotle's alogical half is above all the seat of psychic phenomena open to reason, that is to say the seat of emotional responses
such as fear and anger. Plutarch saw correctly that the alogical
half of Aristotle's bipartite soul is not closed to reason and therefore
is to be distinguished from non-cognitive faculties of nutrition and
sensation. But he erred in thinking that the alogical half could be
created simply by collapsing together the spirited and appetitive
parts of the tripartite soul (*Mor.* 442^b). It was first necessary to
mark off emotional responses from bodily drives and to collect them
together in the alogical half as the sphere of human excellence.

The spirited part (*thymoeides*) of the tripartite soul is not connected with bodily drives such as hunger and thirst, but it does seem
to be connected with non-cognitive behaviour appropriate to
animals and so to be just as complex, not to say confused, a psychic
part as the appetitive part. When Socrates tries to establish the
independent existence of the spirited part, he associates it with anger
(*orgê* 440^{a}5, *orgizesthai* ^{c}2). He refers to the disgust of Leontius
(439^{e}9), the self-reproaches of a man in the grip of desire (440^{b}1),
and the rage of a man thinking himself treated unjustly (440^{c}7).
These examples suggest that the spirited part is to be thought of as
the seat of certain typically human emotions and this suggestion
seems to be confirmed by the *Topics*, which not only locates anger
in the spirited part (126^{a}10) but also is quite clear that being angry
essentially involves the thought of outrage (127^{b}30-1). In other
words the spirited part is connected with cognitive behaviour not
open to animals lacking the capacity of moral assessment (cf. *Pol.*
1253^{a}14-18).[1] Accordingly when Socrates turns to mark off the
spirited part from the reasoning part, he does not do so by referring

---

[1] This is not to say that all emotions assigned to the spirited part of the
tripartite soul involve moral assessment in the way that anger does. Fear, for
example, may be grouped together with anger in the spirited part (*Top.* 126^{a}8-9),
but it does not seem to be so closely tied to moral assessment. For while the
efficient cause of anger is the thought of injustice or outrage (see above, Chapter
One, Section 1), the efficient cause of fear may be simply the thought that
something painful or destructive is imminent. When we focus upon Socrates'
remarks in *Republic* 439^{e}6-440^{d}3, we may want to emphasise the connection
of the spirited part with anger and moral assessment. When we widen our
horizons and think of the spirited part in connection with fear as well as anger,
we may want to speak more generally of a connection between the spirited part
and cognitive emotion. But either way the spirited part is connected with
intelligent behaviour peculiar to thinking creatures.

all modes of cognition to the reasoning part. But what he does do is startling in its own way and a source of difficulty for anyone who wants to see a clear anticipation of Aristotle's political and moral psychology in tripartition. First, Socrates accepts Glaucon's suggestion that the spirited part is different from the reasoning part and that this can be readily seen in the fact that spirit (*thymos*) occurs straightway in children, while reason is never acquired by some and acquired by many only late in life (441^a7-^b1). Then Socrates adds that further support of Glaucon's position is to be seen in the case of animals (441^b2-3). Presumably Socrates means that animals are like children in being full of spirit and lacking in reason. The difficulty with these remarks is not the refusal of reason or calculation (*logismos*) to children and even many adults. It is quite plausible to hold that young children and even many adults lack the capacity to deliberate. Indeed, the refusal of reason or deliberative capacity to a significant group of human beings was to become the crux of Aristotle's justification of slavery.[1] Rather, the difficulty is the connection of the spirited part with animal behaviour. For while the previous remarks of Socrates had encouraged us to think of the spirited part in terms of emotional responses based upon moral assessments and therefore peculiar to human beings, now Socrates' reference to animals seems to extend the sphere of the spirited part to cover the spirited reactions of animals. In itself, of course, such an extension is unobjectionable and even to be expected. The word 'spirit' (*thymos*) is ambiguous in that it can be used in reference to both the angry responses of human beings and the spirited reactions of animals.[2] Furthermore, Socrates' earlier discussion of the temperament requisite in guardians foreshadows this extension of the spirited part. For in pinning down the temperament suitable to guardians, Socrates introduces a well-bred hound (375^a2-^e2), and while Socrates is clear that this hound is a model (375^d5), he does suggest that there is no significant difference between the spirited nature of a noble youth and a well-bred hound (375^a2-3). Our point, then, is not that the spirited part cannot be extended to include animal behaviour or even that we are surprised by this extension in the fourth book of the *Republic*. It is rather that such an extension takes the spirited part beyond the sphere of human action

[1] See below Chapter Three, Section 3.
[2] See my 'Aristotle: Animals, Emotion and Moral Virtue', *Arethusa* 4 (1971) 144.

(*praxis*) to the realm of animal behaviour. Either non-cognitive reactions typical of animals are attributed to the spirited part or alternatively animals are allowed a share in emotional response and so in cognitive behaviour.[1] For an Aristotelian neither alternative is a happy one. The latter allows animals a share in the judgments and assessments peculiar to human beings in relation to animals (*Pol.* 1253ª14–18),[2] while the former mixes non-cognitive reactions with human actions (*EN* 1139ª19-20) and therefore obscures the primary importance of emotional response as a cognitive and peculiarly human mode of behaviour.

We can conclude that bipartition is not only different from but also an advance over tripartition as set forth in the *Republic*. By assigning emotions to all three psychic parts, tripartition fails to make clear a fundamental distinction between emotional response and reasoned deliberation. And by associating the appetitive and spirited parts with bodily drives and animal behaviour, it fails to offer a peculiarly human psychology for use in political and ethical investigation. Aristotle's bipartite psychology avoids these faults. It collects together emotional responses and offers a dichotomy which focuses on two fundamental modes of human behaviour. This is something new—a much improved political and ethical psychology, whose development was preceded and made possible by the Academic investigation of emotion.[3]

[1] Socrates might opt for the latter alternative. See below, Chapter Four, Section 1 on *Laches* 197ª6–ᶜ1. Here it need only be observed that formulating these alternatives depends upon recognising the essential involvement of cognition in emotional response and therefore upon an understanding of emotion which did not arise in the Academy before the period of Plato's *Philebus*.

[2] In this passage from the *Politics* Aristotle treats speech (1253ª14) and the perception of right and wrong (1253ª16-17) as relative properties (1253ª16) because they are not peculiar to man in relation to the gods (cf. *De An.* 414ᵇ18–19) but only in relation to animals whose nature extends only as far as an *aisthêsis* or sensation of pleasure and pain (1253ª12–13).

[3] This is not to say that bipartition was a kind of wonder-working psychology whose powers of elucidation always exceeded those of tripartition. An important example is moral weakness. At first glance it may seem that bipartition is especially suited for elucidating cases of moral weakness. When we consider a man who does not abide by his *logismos* on account of a regrettable *pathos* (*EN* 1145ᵇ10–13), we can describe his behaviour as a victory of the alogical half over the logical half. But on closer inspection we see that bad emotions and desires may be opposed not only to the reflections and calculations of the logical half but also to an emotion like shame. In such a case

4. *Different from tripartition as a developing biological psychology*

Tripartition as formulated in the *Republic* made considerable room for bodily drives and animal behaviour, but it never offered a psychic part totally divorced from cognitive capacity.[1] To be sure calculation is assigned entirely to the reasoning part of the soul, that part whereby a man calculates (*logizesthai* 439^d5; cf. 602^d9-^e2) and comes through deliberation to a reasoned conclusion. But not all judgment and opinion belong to the reasoning part. The spirited part is associated with typical human emotions like anger and fear which are cognitive phenomena involving the thought of outrage and imminent danger (*Rep.* 440^a5-^d3, Ar., *Top.* 126^a8-10, 127^b30-1). The appetitive part is associated primarily with bodily drives, but it is also connected with avaricious desires which do not depend

[1] In arguing that all three members of the tripartite soul as presented in the *Republic* are cognitive, I am concerned to counter the view of, e.g., N. Murphy (*The Interpretation of Plato's Republic* [Oxford 1951]) who describes the *logistikon* as 'the general source of judgment and belief and conviction' (33; cf. 38, 40, 122) and who associates the lower psychic elements when functioning apart from the *logistikon* with mere 'automatic action' (36; cf. M. O'Brien, *The Socratic Paradoxes and the Greek Mind* [Chapel Hill 1967] 152 who connects the lower elements with 'blind tendencies'). However, I am not endorsing the view of Graeser (*Probleme* 21-6, 43, 89; cf. Saunders, 'Structure' 40-1) who wants to align the spirited part as presented in the *Republic* and *Phaedrus* with the world of becoming and opinion in the technical sense set forth in the fifth book of the *Republic*. Graeser is, I think, over-impressed by the possibilities of a 'strenge Koordinierung von Sein, Denken, Tugend und Bios' (*Probleme* 22; cf. 26).

---

the dichotomy of bipartition does not coincide neatly with the battle line of moral weakness. Shame belongs to the alogical half, so that the tension of moral weakness finds expression within the alogical half. Indeed in this particular case tripartition may appear to be a more suitable framework. At least in the *Republic* shame is situated in the *logistikon* (571^c9, 606^c3-6), so that when a desire to raise a laugh is opposed by reason and shame (606^c3-6) the battle line of psychic conflict conforms to a division between psychic parts. What should be underlined is that Aristotle is not blind to the limitations of his political-ethical psychology. He does not employ it when he seeks to determine the function of man (see above, this chapter, Section 2) and is quite prepared to use his biological psychology to explain the tension of moral weakness as a conflict of opposed *orexeis* (*De An.* 433^b5; on *EN* 1147^a31-4 see G. Santas, 'Aristotle on Practical Inference, the Explanation of Action, and Akrasia', *Phronesis* 14 [1969] 179-80). But Aristotle also recognises the improvements involved in his newly developed bipartite psychology and therefore makes it fundamental to his political and ethical investigations.

upon a bodily cause but upon an evaluation (*Rep.* 553^{c}5, 554^{a}2,^{b}2, 580^{e}5–581^{a}7, 590^{b}7–8). Moreover the analogy between city and individual seems to necessitate distributing opinion across all three psychic parts. If the structures of the city and the soul are the same (435^{b}9–^{c}2, ^{e}1–3, 441^{c}4–7) and if the ruling, warrior and merchant classes within the city are composed of thinking individuals who hold opinions of various kinds, then by analogy each of the three psychic parts will have some share in opinion. Indeed, the analogy between city and individual encourages Socrates to explain the temperance of an individual as a common opinion shared by all three psychic parts. Just as a city is temperate when the rulers and the ruled hold the same opinion (*doxa*) concerning who should rule (431^{d}9–^{e}2, 433^{c}6–7), so an individual is temperate when the ruling and ruled psychic elements hold a common opinion concerning who ought to rule (442^{c}10–^{d}1).[1]

Attributing some measure of cognition to all three psychic parts is to be expected in a psychology intended for political and ethical discussion. Human behaviour as against animal behaviour is cognitive, so that a psychological framework based primarily upon different modes of human behaviour will distribute cognition across psychic parts. This is not true of a psychology adapted for biological study. Aristotle's own biological psychology is an obvious example. It marks off intelligence (*nous*)—that faculty whereby the soul thinks and judges (*De An.* 414^{b}18–19, 415^{a}7–9, 427^{b}6–14). In comparison with this biological psychology, the tripartite psychology employed

---

[1] The analogy between city and individual recurs in the tenth book (605^{b}5–8, 608^{b}1) where Socrates works with a bipartite version of tripartition and criticises mimetic poetry on the grounds that it traffics with an inferior part of the mind (603^{b}9–^{c}2). To support this criticism, Socrates first relates mimetic poetry to visual illusions which are said to work on an inferior part of man's soul (605^{a}10–^{b}2) and to be the occasion for opinions opposed to those arising from the calculations of the reasoning part (602^{e}4–603^{a}2). Then Socrates goes on to argue that mimetic poetry nurtures the worst part of the soul and destroys the reasoning part (605^{b}3–5). Socrates is not suggesting that a steady diet of mimetic poetry destroys all cognitive capacity. Since the reasoning part is not the *locus* of all thought and opinion, Socrates can say in a straightforward way that mimetic poetry destroys the reasoning part without suggesting that habitués of poetry are in danger of being reduced to animals. Socrates' point is simply that excessive exposure to mimetic poetry habituates a man to act upon the unreflective judgments characteristic of certain emotional responses and therefore to fail to deliberate (*bouleuesthai* 604^{e}5) about how best to handle particular situations.

in Plato's *Timaeus* is certainly not a fully-developed biological psychology. In nomenclature and certain other respects it remains close to tripartition as advanced in the *Republic*. But the tripartite psychology of the *Timaeus* differs in significant ways from that of the *Republic*, and despite scholarly opinion these differences should not be construed as a step towards Aristotle's political and ethical psychology but rather toward his biological psychology.[1] Of course, it is true that the distinction drawn in the *Timaeus* between immortal and mortal parts of the human soul (41^c6-^d3, 42^d7, 43^a4-5, 69^c5-8, 72^d4) has the effect of formulating a bipartite version of tripartition which groups together the spirited and appetitive parts in opposition to the reasoning part. Out of all context this grouping might be viewed as an anticipation of Aristotle's political and ethical dichotomy, but within the *Timaeus* the grouping seems more naturally construed as a preliminary yet important step in the development of a purely biological psychology. For the immortal part of the soul seems to be conceived of as a locus of cognition and therefore to be an anticipation of Aristotle's biological faculty of intelligence. The immortal part is said to be mixed in much the same way (41^d6) as the World Soul, whose revolutions are associated with thoughts (90^c7-^d1) and are said to constitute intelligent life (36^e4). Accordingly the World Soul is called *nous* or intelligence by Timaios (47^b7) and is even connected by Aristotle with his own biological faculty of intelligence (*De An.* 407^a3-5).[2] If Aristotle is correct that Timaios wished the World Soul to be something like his own biological faculty and if the parallelism and kinship (47^b8, 90^c8) between World Soul and immortal part can be pressed, then the immortal part can be construed as a faculty of cognition and

[1] For the view that the *Timaeus* represents a step on the way to Aristotle's moral dichotomy, see Rees, 'Bipartition' 113 and Graeser, *Probleme* 70, 108. For the *Timaeus* as a step toward Aristotle's biological psychology, see F. Solmsen, 'Antecedents of Aristotle's Psychology and Scale of Beings', *American Journal of Philology* 76 (1955) 153-7, 160-2. Solmsen is clear that a psychological framework useful in biological discussions does not enjoy the same utility in ethical matters and vice versa (150). On the way that a biological point of view shapes the exposition of the *Timaeus* see O'Brien, *Paradoxes* 170-1.

[2] Hicks (*De Anima* 255), notes Aristotle's cautious mode of expression. Aristotle does not claim an exact correspondence between his own biological faculty of *nous* and the World Soul. But he certainly thinks that Timaios is aiming at something like this biological faculty. On the conjunction of *kaloumenos* with *nous* (407^a4-5) to indicate that *nous* is being used in the sense in which Aristotle uses the word, cf. 429^a22, 432^b26 and see the note of Hicks 480.

called with some justification an anticipation of Aristotle's biological faculty of *nous*.

Perhaps the most important passage for understanding tripartition in the *Timaeus* occurs when Timaios discusses the creation and location of the mortal parts of the soul. The passage is not altogether clear and unambiguous, but it may be said to point towards a biological psychology that collects all cognition within one psychic part. The generated gods, Timaios relates, received from the demiurge the immortal part of the soul and created for this immortal part both a body and a mortal soul having within itself terrible and necessary affections: pleasure and pain, confidence and fear, spirit and expectation, mixed together with irrational sensation and venturesome desire (69^{c}5–^{d}6). Timaios' words recall an earlier passage in which the demiurge is made to address the immortal parts of the soul and to depict desire, fear, spirit and their opposites as riotous and irrational feelings following upon bodily sensation and resulting from fire, water, air, and earth (42^{a}3–^{b}1, ^{c}5–^{d}1). Since this earlier passage seems to oppose the immortal part of the soul to feelings and reactions caused by bodily affections, the later passage, too, may be thought to concern itself with pleasant and painful bodily sensations that prompt a creature to react in one way or another. In other words, the mortal part of the soul may be thought to include phenomena assigned by Aristotle to his biological faculty of sensation and not to include cognitions which would be assigned by Aristotle to intelligence.[1] This interpretation is plausible, but it must be admitted that the idea of unwise counsellors (69^{d}3) is compatible with false opinions and that the characterisation of spirit as difficult to dissuade (69^{d}3) suggests cognitive

[1] On the *Timaeus* and the biological faculty of *aisthêsis* see my 'On the Antecedents of Aristotle's Bipartite Psychology', *Greek, Roman and Byzantine Studies* 11 (1970) 246–8. Here two related points may be briefly recalled. First, the *Timaeus* does not avoid serious confusion concerning *aisthêsis*. Sometimes sensation is associated with the immortal part of the soul, sometimes with the mortal, and sometimes with both. Given the biological interests of the *Timaeus*, *aisthêsis* cannot be ignored, but tripartition or its bipartite version has not been sufficiently modified to deal with this biological function (cf. Solmsen, 'Antecedents' 154–5). Secondly, when Aristotle criticises those who divide the soul into logical and alogical halves and says that the *aisthêtikon* cannot be classified easily as either logical or alogical (*De An.* 432^{a}26–31), he is not concerned with the dichotomy implicit in the *Laws* and fully formulated in his own political and ethical treatises. Rather he is thinking of a bipartite version of tripartition such as Plato employed in the *Timaeus* to handle biological material.

emotion which is in principle at least open to persuasion even when it resists the appeals of reasoned argument.[1] Furthermore, expectation (*elpis*) is understood most naturally as a kind of opinion concerning the future (cf. *Phil.* 32^{b}9–^{c}2), and the subsequent description of the spirited part of the mortal soul as that part which listens to reason (70^{a}5) suggests a cognitive element that heeds reasoned advice in the way that a child listens to his father (cf. Ar., *EN* 1102^{b}31–2). We must admit, I think, that this portion of the *Timaeus* is not altogether clear concerning the cognitive status of the mortal parts of the soul. But when we consider what Timaios goes on to say concerning the spirited part of the mortal soul, we can say that this portion of the *Timaeus* tends towards a biological psychology that collects together all cognition. For in discussing the spirited part and its relationship to the heart, Timaios not only gives a physiological description of the activity of spirit (70^{b}3, ^{c}3) but also refers the evaluative judgment involved in anger to the immortal part of the soul. *Logos* or reason is said to announce that an unjust act has taken place and spirit is said to boil (70^{b}3–5). The evaluation essential to the emotion of anger is referred to the immortal or reasoning part,[2] and we may suppose that when Timaios speaks of the leaping of the heart upon the expectation of danger (70^{c}1–2), the opinion of imminent danger belongs to the immortal soul and the accompanying painful feelings to the mortal soul.

It seems, then, that the reasoning part of the tripartite soul as presented in the *Timaeus* is on the way to becoming a locus of cognition similar to Aristotle's biological faculty of *nous*. For the history of biological psychology, this is a matter of considerable significance.

[1] The adjective *dysparamythêtos* or 'difficult-to-persuade' (69^{d}3) suggests the difficulty but not the (conceptual) impossibility of *paramythia* or persuasive admonition. For *paramythia* and cognates in the sense of persuasive admonition, cf. *Laws* 720^{a}1, 854^{a}6, 885^{b}3, 899^{d}6 and *Rep.* 476^{e}1 where *paramytheisthai* is used in conjunction with *peithein* (to persuade) to denote winning over a man who is angered and thinks others quite wrong.

[2] Galen (*Hipp. et Plat.* 5.498 K) paraphrases *Timaeus* 70^{b}5 and adds that believing (*doxazein*) injustice has occurred belongs to the *logistikon*. Galen's addition seems to be correct. Just as the *De Anima* recognises that anger involves a boiling of the blood in the region of the heart (403^{a}31) and yet is quite clear in restricting judgment and evaluation to the faculty of intelligence, so the *Timaeus* seems to recognise that being angry involves a leaping of the heart and boiling of *thymos* (70^{b}3, ^{c}1–2) and that these physiological phenomena are to be distinguished from the judgment of injustice (70^{b}3–5) which belongs to the *logistikon* now moving towards a biological faculty of cognition.

For our own investigation, it is perhaps of even greater importance that the movement of the *Timaeus* towards a biological psychology is in no way at odds with the movement of the *Laws* away from tripartition and towards bipartition as a more satisfactory political and ethical psychology. For biological purposes and in particular for classifying different kinds of life it is useful to locate all cognition within a single faculty of intelligence.[1] But for political and ethical

---

[1] It is worth mentioning that the *Timaeus* is not only moving toward a biological psychology which locates all cognition in a single psychic faculty but also moving toward a *scala naturae* not unlike the *scala* set forth in Aristotle's *De Anima*. Land animals, we are told, came into being from men who made no use of philosophy and did not study the heavens, because they had ceased to use the revolutions in the head and had come to follow the parts of soul located in the breast (91e2–6). This passage does not cover all kinds of animals. It explains the generation of land animals by reference to transmigration and does not concern itself with birds whose mode of life is somewhat higher or fish whose mode of life is somewhat lower than that of land animals (91d6–e1, 92a7–c1). Furthermore, the passage does not say that animals have only the two lower and mortal parts of the soul and so does not formulate a *scala naturae* which withholds clearly and completely the reasoning part from animals. Rather the passage says only that animals no longer use the immortal soul whose revolutions are crushed together within an elongated head (91e8–92a2). Still, the passage does suggest that the life of land animals is fundamentally different from the intelligent life of human beings and therefore may be said to recall the views of Alkmaion (DK 24A5) and to look forward to Aristotle's *scala naturae* and the attribution of sensation without cognition to animals (*De An.* 413b1–10, 414a33–b3, 415a3–6, 427b6–16, 434a30). Of equal significance is the fact that the *Timaeus* associates the appetitive part with nutrition and plant life. The appetitive part, we are told, is concerned with food and drink and situated between the midriff and the boundary towards the navel, where it feeds at a kind of manger (70d7–e5). In this passage the appetitive part is closely tied to the basic life-function of nutrition, so that it is not surprising to find it attributed later to plants (77b3–4) which Aristotle characterises as possessing the nutritive capacity alone (*De An.* 413a25–b1, 414a33, 434a22–6). This is not to say that the appetitive part of the *Timaeus* can be identified with Aristotle's biological faculty of nutrition. Its connection with certain peculiar sensations (77a4–5, b5–6) is sufficient to distinguish it from Aristotle's biological faculty and is perhaps partly responsible for Aristotle's insistence that there is no sixth sense (*De An.* 424b22–425b11). Moreover, the idea of frightening the appetitive part is difficult to reconcile with a biological faculty of nutrition, as is the connection with mantic power (71d3) and with moods such as ill-temper and despondency (87a5). For although such moods may have a physiological cause closely connected with nutritive processes, they characteristically manifest themselves in cognitive behaviour involving gloomy thoughts and grouchy statements. But despite these differences between the appetitive part as presented in the *Timaeus* and Aristotle's biological faculty of nutrition, the appetitive part may be said

purposes such a concentration is not as useful, and it should come as no surprise to find the Athenian stranger in the first book of the *Laws* recalling *Timaeus* 69^{d}3 and indicating the relation of his new political and ethical psychology to the biological psychology incipient in the *Timaeus*.[1] Fear and confidence are introduced explicitly as opinions (*doxai*) and expectation (*elpis*) is declared a common name for opinions concerning the future (644^{c}9–^{d}1). In other words, the Athenian Stranger does not withhold cognition from the lower half of the dichotomy implicit in this portion of the *Laws*. Instead, he exhibits the influence of Academic work on emotional response and recognises the cognitive core of phenomena properly grouped on the lower side of a political and ethical dichotomy. This is not to say that the Stranger is rejecting the movement of the *Timaeus* toward a biological psychology and a biological faculty of cognition. Were he doing biology, the Stranger could be expected to opt for such a psychology and to approve of the psychology ultimately set forth in Aristotle's *De Anima*. But he is not doing biology and therefore does not opt for biological divisions. He makes clear his position in regard to tripartition as an incipient biological psychology and works with an ethical dichotomy which distributes cognition across its major division.

---

[1] The occurrence of the phrase 'unwise counsellors' at both *Timaeus* 69^{d}3 and *Laws* 644^{c}6–7 is striking. But it must be cautioned that in the *Timaeus* the phrase is associated with fear and confidence, while in the *Laws* it is associated with pleasure and pain. The *Laws* passage seems to offer a reminiscence and not a carefully controlled quote.

---

to be moving toward Aristotle's biological faculty and to be part of an incipient *scala naturae*, which was soon to be formulated by Aristotle in terms of his own biological psychology.

CHAPTER THREE

Consequences for Political Theory

1. *Moral education*

The investigation of emotion and subsequent development of a new and peculiarly human psychology led among other things to a new formulation of educational theory. This is evident in the *Politics* where Aristotle not only divides the soul into alogical and logical halves but also relates this division to a temporal distinction. The alogical half is said to be prior in generation to the logical half and also said to be educated in advance of the logical half (1334^b21–8; cf. 1338^b4–5). There is nothing obscure or unusual about these remarks. Aristotle holds that young persons are characterised by emotional response and not by reasoned reflection. He also holds that emotions are cognitive and therefore open to moral education. A young person can be taught principles which will guide his responses even though his principles are not yet fully understood. This is, of course, very much a matter of common sense. Parents who have never studied philosophical psychology make sure their children learn rules of good conduct and yet do not expect them to explain the rules by means of reasoned argumentation. But if this is a matter of common sense, it is also a matter of some importance. For tripartition as employed in Plato's *Republic* was inadequate to support and explain the educational system set forth in this dialogue. Psychological theory lagged behind educational theory and caught up only when emotions were focused upon and their relationship to reason formulated in a new political and ethical psychology.

In the *Republic* Plato was quite emphatic that moral education should begin straightway from youth (378^d1, 386^a2, 395^c4, 401^d1), that moral values should be imparted before the age of reasoned understanding (402^a2–4). Moreover, he recognised that the capacity to reason comes comparatively late in life and called upon this fact to justify marking off the reasoning part of the soul from the spirited part (*Rep.* 441^a7–$^b1$). But he could not press this argument to say that the reasoning part is posterior in generation and therefore educated after the spirited and appetitive parts. For not all desires

45

and emotions are assigned to the two lower psychic parts. In particular, shame, an emotion of considerable importance in the training of young people (cf. *Rep.* 378^{c}2, 388^{d}6) belongs to the reasoning part of the tripartite soul as presented in the *Republic* (571^{c}9, 606^{c}3–6). Furthermore, when Plato does relate tripartition to education, he does not refer to all three psychic parts. The reasoning and spirited parts are connected with musical and gymnastic education, and the appetitive part is passed over in silence (411^{e}4–412^{a}2, 441^{e}8–442^{a}2). This may be due to the fact that the appetitive part is above all the seat of hunger and thirst (437^{d}3–4) and therefore the seat of bodily drives which can be controlled or repressed, but which are not open to moral education in the way that cognitive emotions are.[1] Still, bodily drives do not exhaust the contents of the appetitive part. Greed, a cognitive desire of considerable importance, belongs to this psychic part (580^{e}5–581^{a}7). A system of moral education which does not address itself to greed is seriously deficient and in discussing musical education Plato is quite prepared to criticise Homer for presenting mercenary and grasping characters (390^{e}7–391^{a}2). But when he applies his tripartite psychology to educational theory, he ignores the appetitive part and so seems to ignore avaricious feelings. Perhaps we can conclude that tripartition does not readily support the theory of education advanced in the *Republic* and more generally that the divisions of tripartition do not conform to everyday educational practice. A new psychology was needed and was in the process of development when Plato wrote the *Laws*. Aristotle brought this process to completion. He divided the soul into alogical and logical halves and in so doing added a clear psychological basis to educational theory. Desires and emotional responses were brought together in a single psychic half which was seen to be prior in generation and therefore prior in education.

Here a word of caution is in order. Aristotle is primarily concerned with educating the cognitive side of emotional response, but he does recognise other kinds of habituation. For example, he recommends an early habituation towards cold and justifies this habituation on the grounds that it makes a person healthier and better fitted for military service (1336^{a}12–15). In the *Laws* Plato had noted Spartan institutions which habituate young persons to endure extremes of temperature (633^{c}1–5), and in the *Politics* Aristotle refers to bar-

[1] Cf. A. J. P. Kenny, 'Mental Health in Plato's Republic', *Proceedings of the British Academy* 55 (1969) 235.

barians who immerse newborn infants in cold rivers and Celts who
hardly wrap their infants (1336ᵃ15–18).[1] Such an habituation is not
directly moral, though it does have an effect on moral situations
such as military campaigns. Aristotle is well aware of this and does
not conceal the fact that the sphere of habituation includes bodily
sensations like painful temperatures. Indeed he even recognises
that while animals live mostly by nature, some animals live a little
by habit (1332ᵇ3–4),[2] even though the nature of animals extends no

---

[1] Aristotle is not altogether explicit that the habituation to cold should begin
with new-born infants, but the example of the barbarians and the phrases
'straightway with little children' (1336ᵃ13–14) and 'straightway at the beginning'
(1336ᵃ18–19) seem to allow no other interpretation. W. Newman (*The Politics
of Aristotle* [Oxford 1887–1902] 3.478) points out that in recommending an
habituation of infants to extreme temperatures Aristotle is going beyond Spartan
and Cretan practices and also Plato's *Republic* which contemplates habituation
in respect to heat and cold (404ᵇ1) but speaks only of training children (403ᶜ11),
not 'little' children.

[2] It seems to me easiest and most sensible to interpret Aristotle's remark about
animals (1332ᵇ3–4) as a straightforward recognition of the fact that habituation
does play a role, though a little one, in the lives of animals. Still, it may be
noted that the addition of the phrase beginning with 'a little' (1332ᵇ4) could be
a kind of throw-in. Following Newman, *The Politics* 3.432, we may compare
1332ᵇ3–4 with *Metaph.* 980ᵇ25–8: the other creatures (animals as against men)
live by imaginations and memories, and possess experience a little. The two
passages are similar in structure and wording and may be used to interpret one
another. At least it is possible to construe *Metaph.* 980ᵇ27–8 as a kind of deliberate understatement. Since 980ᵇ28–9 seems to associate experience with
men and 981ᵃ7–9 seems to make experience a matter of holding particular
judgments, it can be argued that Aristotle really wants to say that animals do
not partake of experience. (See Alexander 4.15 and Sir David Ross, *Aristotle's
Metaphysics* [Oxford 1958] 1.117.) 980ᵇ26–7 may be a kind of throw-in such
as we have at *Physics* 226ᵇ27–8 ('or as little as possible' must be a throw-in, for
continuous change can admit no break, however little) and possibly at *De An.*
428ᵇ19 (or 'possessing falsehood as little as possible' may be a throw-in, for it
seems to be contradicted by 418ᵃ12, 427ᵇ12, 428ᵃ11, *Metaph.* 1010ᵇ24—but for
a possible resolution see D. W. Hamlyn, 'Aristotle's Account of Aesthesis in the
De Anima', *Classical Quarterly* N.S. 9 [1959] 11–13, *Aristotle's De Anima*
134–5). These passages suggest that Aristotle threw in occasionally (perhaps to
affect a tentative manner) a qualifier that is not to be pressed. So *Pol.* 1332ᵇ4
may be a kind of throw-in without serious implications. Still, there are degrees
of throwing-in and here the throw-in seems to admit of easy explanation.
Animals are said in ordinary discourse to act in habitual ways, so that Aristotle
throws in a concession to ordinary discourse that in no way implies animals can
partake of the ethical habituation which inculcates moral principles and trains
moral assessment.

farther than pleasant and painful sensations (1253^a12-13). But to attribute some small degree of habituation to animals and to recommend habituation in regard to sensations of cold is not to restrict the habituation of human beings to the sphere of sensations or even to suggest that the habituation of human children is concerned primarily with sensations. Indeed, such a restriction and suggestion would be close to nonsense after the Academic investigation of emotion and the development of a new political and ethical psychology. Aristotle recognised that emotions are cognitive phenomena significantly different from the pleasant and painful sensations which control animal behaviour.[1] He was in no doubt that children are emotional and therefore cognitive beings open to and in need of a training in values. In other words, Aristotle assigned young people an education in moral principles not in spite of, but rather because of their alogical nature.

Among the various influences upon moral character it is the musical *paideia* which is singled out by Aristotle for special treatment because of its unique role in developing morally good habits. Aristotle's position is clear enough. Young persons are not willing to endure anything that is not pleasant (1340^b15-16). Music is naturally pleasant (1340^b16-17) and also imitative of moral character (1340^a18). Young children enjoy the natural and common pleasures of music (1340^a2-4) and at the same time are habituated to enjoy the good characters and noble deeds depicted in rhythm and song (1340^a16-18). There is a slide here, but it is a virtuous slide. Children begin by delighting in the natural or common pleasures of music (1340^a2-5, 1341^a15-16), but soon transfer this delight to the noble characters and actions that are depicted in song and dances. And once they have been habituated to delight in representations of noble character, they have all but acquired a delight in actual noble character (1340^a23-5). That is, a person who has been habituated to enjoy musical depictions of, say, courageous character (1340^a20) has all but acquired the character and is well along the road towards a willing endurance of noble dangers (1338^b31).

This habituation is a training in values that goes far beyond the

---

[1] Of course, the behaviour of animals manifests considerable critical capacity and therefore may be spoken of as discriminating behaviour. But the discriminations of animals remain at the level of *aisthêsis*. They are not cognitive in the sense of propositional judgments open to the persuasion of reasoned *logos*. See below, Chapter Four, Section 1.

sort of habituation that is appropriate to animals. Young children
are to be taught moral principles and towards this end words are
important. Just as Plato disapproved of wordless rhythms on the
grounds that it was difficult to tell what they represent (*Laws*
669^{e}1–4), so Aristotle disapproved of flutes which make the usage
of words impossible (1341^{a}24–5). The musical *paideia* is not concerned with developing a pattern of reactions to pleasant and painful sensations, but rather with virtue and the ability to make correct
assessments (1340^{a}15–18). This is, of course, the position of the
Laws. *Paideia* is the initial acquisition of virtue by children. Young
people are first habituated to love and to hate correctly, so that later
when they have acquired the ability to deliberate and reflect there
will be a symphony between habituated preferences and what
reasoning shows to be good (653^{b}1–6). Aristotle's contribution is
not to alter but rather to formulate this fundamental position. He
follows Plato in referring virtue to properly trained loves and hates
(*Laws* 653^{b}2–3, *Pol.* 1340^{a}15). Only he improves, or at least
sharpens, the Platonic position by formally dividing the soul into
alogical and logical halves and by arguing that first the alogical half
is habituated correctly and then this habituation is confirmed by the
reflections of the logical half. We may conclude that Aristotle along
with the other members of the Academy recognised that educational
theory demands an adequate human psychology. He saw clearly the
inadequacies of tripartition and drawing upon the Academic investigation of emotion developed a new human psychology which
could explain and justify different stages in moral education.

2. *The imperfection of young people*

Focusing upon emotional behaviour and making precise the relationship between emotion and reasoned reflection resulted not only
in an improved formulation of educational theory but also in a
natural or psychological explanation of the position of young people,
slaves and women within the Greek city-state. Justifying the subordinate role of any large group within a political community is in
itself always a matter of considerable interest, but Aristotle's remarks have an additional historical interest in that they are quite
consciously intended to support the claim of Gorgias that different
groups within society have different roles and virtues (1260^{a}27–8;

cf. Plato, *Meno* 71ᶜ5–72ᵃ5). Aristotle accepted Plato's demand that a difference in role be tied to a relevant difference in nature or capacity (*Rep.* 454ᶜ7–ᵈ1) and at the same time defended the *status quo* of much of Greek society.

After our preceding remarks on education the case of young people should be intelligible enough. Aristotle is impressed by an observable correlation between youth and emotion. He thinks that young people tend to behave emotionally and without reflection. He formulates this by saying that the alogical half of the soul is prior in generation, and is quite prepared to say that intellectual development is something that cannot be hurried. Indeed Aristotle holds that a man's mental maturity comes only in the fiftieth year and therefore is quite distinct from maturity of body occurring in the thirty-seventh year (1335ᵃ29, ᵇ34–5). In practical terms this means that young people cannot be morally perfect. Plato expresses this idea in the *Laws* when he distinguishes the perfect (*teleos*) man of total virtue (*sympasa aretê*) from the younger person who has been trained in loves and hates (653ᵃ5–ᶜ4). In the *Politics* Aristotle makes this view his own. He holds that a child is imperfect (*atelês*) in regard to deliberative capacity (1260ᵃ13–14, cf. 1259ᵇ4, 1260ᵃ31, 1275ᵃ17, 1339ᵃ31) and therefore is not to be identified with the best man (1333ᵃ12, 1334ᵃ13). We may compare the *Rhetoric* which is like the *Politics* in recognising a difference between the age of mental and the age of physical maturity (1390ᵇ9–11), and which characterises young persons in part by a general failure to live by *logismos* (1389ᵃ33–4). However, the *Rhetoric* is quite clear that young people can be educated so as to acquire an *êthos* or established disposition to act with a view to what is noble (1389ᵃ28–35). This disposition is virtue (1389ᵃ35), though not the more perfect virtue of the mature man whose actions are guided both by *êthos* and by *logismos*. Much as Plato associates virtue with the initial education of young people (*Laws* 653ᵇ1–2), so Aristotle is prepared to associate virtue with the moral training of youth. This is clear not only in the *Rhetoric*'s discussion of different ages and in the *Politics*' discussion of musical education (1340ᵃ15), but also in the *Ethics* where Aristotle suggests a temporal difference between acquiring virtues of the alogical and logical halves of the soul (1103ᵃ17) and then goes on to discuss the acquisition of moral virtues (1103ᵃ19). According to Aristotle they arise neither by nature nor contrary to nature. Men are naturally disposed to receive them and are perfected through habituation (1103ᵃ23-6). Aristotle's point is straight-forward.[1] Correct education (1104ᵇ13) is a moral training in values which perfects (1103ᵃ25) man's alogical side, so that a man makes correct assessments (1104ᵇ1) and chooses proper actions for their own sakes (1105ᵃ32). By habituation lawgivers hope to make men good (1103ᵇ3-4). Of course, this goodness is not the perfected dis-position that Plato had referred to as total virtue. Aristotle is not unaware of this and later says that virtue in the strict sense does not arise without practical wisdom (1144ᵇ16-17). But if virtue in the strict sense is always found together with (*meta*) the *orthos logos* that is practical wisdom (1144ᵇ27-8), there is also a humbler con-dition which Aristotle does not hesitate to label virtue (*Pol.* 1340ᵃ15, *Rhet.* 1389ᵃ35, *EN* 1103ᵃ24). It is an *êthos* (*Pol.* 1339ᵃ24, *Rhet.* 1389ᵃ33, *EN* 1179ᵇ29) which is acquired through an early training of loves and hates and which is a prerequisite (*EN* 1179ᵇ24, 29-30) for the subsequent acquisition of total virtue. In Aristotelian termi-

---

[1] In an interesting article ('Aristotle on the Role of Intellect in Virtue', *Proceedings of the Aristotelian Society* 74 [1973-4] 120) R. Sorabji comments on this portion of *EN* 2. He first suggests that Aristotle expresses himself in a mis-leading way and then allows that perhaps Aristotle is thinking in Platonic terms and recognising the temporal priority of virtue acquired through habituation. The latter interpretation seems to me correct and important. Just as Aristotle's political-ethical psychology is a formulation of the dichotomy operative in Plato's *Laws*, so Aristotle's views on virtue have their antecedents in the *Laws*. This is especially clear in the opening pages of *EN* 2. When Aristotle calls pleasure and pain the whole concern of virtue and political science (1105ᵃ10-12), he is recalling *Laws* 636ᵈ5-7, where the Athenian Stranger says that almost the whole investigation of men studying law is concerned with pleasures and pains. When Aristotle speaks of men who pursue pleasures which they ought not to, at times they ought not to and in a manner they ought not to (1104ᵇ22-3) he is using language which is at least similar to that of *Laws* 636ᵈ8-ᵉ1, and when he qualifies the demand that courageous men delight in endurance and asks only that they not be pained (1104ᵇ7-8), he is adding a qualification which may be compared with *Laws* 862ᵈ7. And finally when Aristotle connects *paideia* with pleasure and pain and urges that training begin straightway from childhood (1104ᵇ11-13), he names Plato and is thinking of *Laws* 653ᵃ5-ᶜ4 (cf. 635ᵇ2-ᵈ7, 643ᵇ4-644ᵇ4). Such reminiscences are more than casual. They are indications that Aristotle's own views on virtue and moral education are similar to those advanced in the *Laws*. Accordingly we should not be surprised that Aristotle's opening remarks in *EN* 2 have a Platonic ring. Far from being misleading, they help us see Aristotle's doctrine of virtue against the background of Plato's *Laws* and the distinction between total virtue appropriate to mature men and habituated virtue appropriate to younger persons trained in loves and hates.

nology it is a perfected state of man's alogical side and the goal of
moral *paideia*.[1]

The political application of all this to young people is that they
can be refused positions of authority. Having not yet reached
intellectual maturity and developed practical wisdom they lack the
perfect (*telea*) virtue which is demanded of a man in authority
(1260^a17-18, cf. 1276^b34). The virtue of the ruler is the virtue of the
best man (1333^a11-12; cf. 1277^a13-16). This virtue a younger
person does not have. Of course, this does not mean that a young
person must be entirely without virtue and in no sense a good
citizen.[2] Moral *paideia* may have taught him good principles and
given him practice in applying them, but it cannot have taught him
to reason well and in particular to explain and defend his moral
principles. Such teaching must await the development of deliberative capacity. It follows that Aristotle can reserve authority for
older persons without violating the principle of equal status for like
people (1332^b27). The distinction between ruler and ruled is
grounded upon an educational difference (cf. 1332^b12-16, $b41-$
1333^a2) which is in turn grounded upon a natural or psychological
difference between young and mature men. A happy consequence
is that young persons will have to earn full citizenship. They will
serve in the army before they rule and generally will engage in a
variety of tasks which test their moral fibre and fitness to rule. But
this consequence is not the primary justification for withholding

[1] I do not think that there is any difficulty in saying that a man's alogical side
may be perfected even at a time when his logical side remains imperfect. Of
course, such a man does not possess in himself the perfect reason or practical
wisdom to which his alogical or emotional side should listen. But ideally he has
been educated under law which is an expression of practical wisdom (*Rhet.*
1389^a29, *EN* 1180^a14-24, $^b23-8$) and in any case has acquired a disposition
which is obedient to the reasoned guidance of a father, tutor or ruler. Moreover,
Aristotle views the development of full moral perfection as a two-step process.
The first step does not result in total virtue, but it is a process which must be
worked through first (*EN* 1179^b24) and which ends in a state of habituated
perfection (*EN* 1103^a25). This may be a low-level perfection, but it is a perfection which completes the process of moral *paideia*, which is the training of
man's alogical side.

[2] Cf. *Pol.* 1277^b25-7 where Aristotle says 'practical wisdom is the only virtue
peculiar to a ruler, for the other virtues seem to be necessary alike for ruler and
ruled'. A younger person cannot qualify as a ruler, because he cannot acquire
practical wisdom. But properly educated he can acquire other virtues and serve
the state well in a subordinate role.

authority from young people. Rather it is the distinction between emotional and reasoning halves of the soul which justifies Aristotle in assigning young people a subordinate role of obedience to men of mature intellect.

3. *Natural slaves*

Aristotle's account of the natural slave is also grounded firmly upon his new political-ethical psychology, so that a proper understanding of this psychology goes a long way towards rendering intelligible Aristotle's view of slavery. This is especially true in regard to the question whether slaves qualify as human beings.[1] Why anyone should think that Aristotle's account involves difficulties concerning the humanity of slaves is clear enough. In the *Politics* Aristotle emphasises the capacity of a slave for bodily labour (1252^a33, 1254^b18, 25, 1258^b38, 1259^b26) and withholds completely the capacity to deliberate (1260^a12). While a master is able to look ahead thoughtfully ($1252^a31–2$) and so plan a course of action, a slave cannot. It is to his advantage to be ruled and guided by a master (1252^a34, 1254^b19, 1278^b34). The slave is even said to differ from his master to the same extent that body differs from soul and beast from man ($1254^b16–17$). In regard to useful activity there seems to be little difference between slaves and tame animals. Both are said to offer bodily aid towards securing the necessities of life ($1254^b24–6$).

These remarks relate closely slaves and animals, so that it is perhaps understandable that difficulties have been felt concerning the humanity of slaves. But Aristotle is quite explicit in classifying slaves as men (1254^a16, $1259^b27–8$), and if we understand clearly how Aristotle's biological psychology differs from his political and ethical dichotomy, we can see rather easily how a slave qualifies as a human being. He has speech, can form propositions and even make moral judgments. He has a cognitive capacity peculiar to men

---

[1] On this question see E. Barker, *The Political Thought of Plato and Aristotle* (New York 1959) 364–5; R. Schlaifer, 'Greek Theories of Slavery from Homer to Aristotle', *Harvard Studies in Classical Philology* 47 (1936) 192–9; O. Gigon, 'Die Sklaverei bei Aristoteles' in *La 'Politique d'Aristote'* (Genève 1964) 247–83; and A. W. H. Adkins, *From the Many to the One* (Ithaca 1970) 211–12.

in relation to other animals (1253ᵇ16)[1] and can be said to have attained the minimum level of cognitive ability required by the biological psychology of any creature that is to be classified as a man. However, the cognitive abilities of a slave have very definite limits. He is said to lack altogether the capacity to deliberate (1260ᵃ–12). This does not mean that a slave is some strange non-cognitive animal whose only performance is bodily. On the contrary Aristotle never refuses slaves a share in the alogical half of the bipartite soul and therefore in the emotional behaviour typical of younger persons and common in adults. What he does refuse slaves is the capacity to deliberate, that is to say the logical half of the dichotomy. Slaves lack the capacity to reflect and think ahead and therefore need to be guided by persons who enjoy this ability. Aristotle can say that the function of a slave is bodily (1254ᵇ18) and can contrast the bodily capacity of a slave with the foresight of a master (1252ᵃ31–3) without committing himself to the view that a slave is in every respect like an animal. The contribution of slaves to the association of men is bodily and so appropriately related to the contribution of domestic animals (1254ᵇ26). But their psychic capacities go beyond the sensations of animals. They possess an alogical or emotional side and therefore cannot be classified as beasts.

A slave is said to lack the capacity for deliberation. This assertion is understandable enough. But what does Aristotle mean when he says that slaves do not possess *logos* but do perceive it (1254ᵇ22–3)? This assertion is curious and has been called 'a truly precarious thesis'.[2] Still, what Aristotle wants to say is, I think, fairly clear. Even though a slave cannot deliberate for himself, he can follow reasoned deliberations and instructions and therefore can be said to perceive or appreciate *logos*. Ignoring Socrates' claims only to question and not to teach (Plato, *Meno* 84ᶜ11–ᵈ1, 85ᵈ3), we might say that Aristotle's natural slave is rather like Meno's boy, who could be led through a geometrical investigation but went wrong or drew a blank when left to his own resources (*Meno* 82ᵉ2–3, 83ᵉ2, 84ᵃ1–2, 85ᵃ4–5). By nature unable to do his own reasoning, a

[1] Speech (1253ᵃ14) and a perception of right and wrong (1253ᵃ16–17) are treated as relative properties (1253ᵃ16) because they are not peculiar to men in relation to the gods (cf. *De An.* 414ᵇ18–19) but only in relation to animals whose nature extends only as far as an *aisthêsis* of pleasure and pain (1253ᵃ12–13).

[2] Gigon, 'Sklaverei' 258. Cf. Cchlaifer ('Greek Theories' 193) who says that 'Aristotle is inconsistent within the limits of one sentence'.

natural slave can at least follow the reasoning of other persons and so is open to instruction of various kinds. Most obviously, he can be instructed in menial skills which may not merit the serious attention of a master (1277^a34-^b7) but which may be said to constitute a kind of slavish *epistêmê* (1255^b22-3) and which are taught to slaves for a fee at Syracuse (1255^b23-5). Further and more important, a slave can appreciate the reasoned reflections of another and alter his emotional responses accordingly. A slave's alogical side, like that of any other person, is open to reasoned persuasion (*EN* 1102^b33-4), so that Aristotle thinks it a mistake to employ only command in dealing with slaves. Instead of depriving slaves of all contact with *logos* or reasoned argumentation, we should admonish (*nouthetein*) them even more than we do children (1260^b5-7) and should not punish them without offering a *logos* which prevents anger by justifying punishment (*Rhet.* 1380^b16-20).

In opposing simple commands and in recommending reasoned admonition, Aristotle is criticising Plato who in the *Laws* (777^e4-778^a5) has the Athenian Stranger warn against spoiling slaves by admonishing them as if they were free men (777^e5-6). According to the Stranger a simple order is the proper mode of address to use in dealing with slaves (777^e6-778^a1). The rationale is clearly practical. A playful manner in dealing with slaves is thought to spoil them and to make life more difficult for both a master and his slaves (778^a1-5). This view is not grounded upon any psychological theory according to which slaves are marked off from free men by reference to a difference in intellectual capacity. Rather the Platonic discussion takes its impetus from a realisation that the handling of slaves at Sparta, Heraclea, Thessaly and Italy has been faulty (776^c6-^d2, 777^c1-5) and from a firm belief that slaves should be well-disposed towards their masters (776^d6). The fact of serious unrest among groups of slaves encourages Plato to suggest that slaves be different in nationality and speech (777^c7-^d2), treated properly (777^d2) and punished whenever it is just to do so (777^e4-5). In this portion of the *Laws* Plato is not motivated by any conviction that slaves are all alike in lacking reason or that there is a class of natural slaves who are marked off clearly from other men by some difference in kind. Instead he recognises how difficult it is to distinguish between slaves and free men (777^b5-7) and never denies that on occasion slaves may be of superior virtue and responsible for the preservation of their masters and their masters' properties (776ᵈ6–ᵉ1).

The Athenian Stranger's remarks concerning slaves and simple orders are closely related to earlier remarks concerning the medical treatment of slaves. When slaves give medical treatment to other slaves they are said neither to give nor to receive an account (*logos*) but simply to order what seems best (720ᶜ3–6, cf. 857ᶜ8). This method is contrasted with the treatment of free men by free doctors. Free doctors are said to engage the patient in dialogue, instruct (*didaskein*) him concerning the nature of his disease and give orders only after persuading the patient to comply (720ᵈ1–ᵉ2, cf. 857ᵈ1–ᵉ1). Something similar to this medical instruction of free men would seem to be what Plato has in mind later when he has the Athenian Stranger warn against admonishing slaves as if they were free men. Slaves are not to be offered an account but rather to be given simple directives in much the same way that a sick slave is given a prescription without explanation. Aristotle, I suspect, was fully aware of the relationship between the Athenian Stranger's remarks on the treatment of ailing slaves and on the proper way to address slaves. He seems to have interpreted the *Laws* in the manner suggested and to have objected to the recommendation of simple prescription or order (*Laws* 720ᶜ5, 778ᵃ1, Ar., *Pol.* 1260ᵇ6) without any accompanying *logos* or account (*Laws* 720ᶜ3, Ar., *Pol.* 1260ᵇ5). Moreover, his objection seems to meet Plato on his own ground in that it seems to be grounded firmly upon the dichotomy implicit in the *Laws*. For this dichotomy recognises that man's emotional side is open to reasoned persuasion and that man's moral character can benefit from reasoned discourse. Children who as yet cannot reason for themselves are to be taught the *logoi* that make up the *Laws* and also similar compositions and unwritten discourses (811ᶜ6–ᵉ5). Persons desiring to rob a temple are urged to enter into conversations with good men (854ᵇ8–ᶜ1) and persons convicted of injustice are to be reformed in part at least through teaching and *logoi* (862ᵈ2, 5). The idea is that a man's desires are open to reasoned persuasion, so that explanations are helpful in controlling a man's desires and forming his moral character. Why, then, withhold this useful method of training and correction from slaves? The answer may lie in the fact that the *Laws* does not advance a doctrine of natural slavery based upon the dichotomy of bipartition. If the goal is to train certain men irrespective of their mental capacities to be obedient slaves, then an account may be harmful. For ultimately there is no reason why men of similar ability should be treated differently and to offer an insufficient account will only evoke a negative response from intelligent men who must be made well-disposed towards their masters. But if a doctrine of natural slavery is formulated not only individual orders but even the all-important call to servitude can be defended and rendered acceptable by a *logos*.

Aristotle, it seems, develops a view of natural slaves based upon the dichotomy implicit in the *Laws* and set forth explicitly in his own ethical and political treatises. Natural slaves lack the capacity to deliberate but possess an emotional side that can appreciate the reasoning of others and therefore is open to correction through reasoned admonition. Finally, it should be noticed that Aristotle's view has the merit of running a middle course between the opposing views recognised by Plato in the *Laws*. It neither allows the possibility of slaves excelling in regard to every virtue (776^d9) nor despises them as if they were animals (777^a4). Instead it seems to take a hint from Homer (*Od.* 17.322) or rather Plato's misquotation to the effect that slaves lack half their wits (777^a1). They lack the capacity to deliberate but are in other respects cognitive creatures. Such a view may not be altogether novel. At least in the *Laws* Klinias is prepared to equate an inability to demonstrate by *logos* with the condition of a slave (966^b1–3). But it seems to be Aristotle who formulated this deficiency in terms of his new political-ethical psychology and made deliberative incapacity the basis of natural slavery.

4. *Women and their subordinate role*

For Aristotle women are the result of a physiological failure at the moment of conception. During the act of procreation male semen attempts to impose its form on female matter. When the semen is altogether successful and gains mastery over the female residue, a male offspring is produced (*GA* 767^b21). But when the semen fails to gain mastery over female matter, perhaps because of some deficiency in heat, then the semen does not impose its form on the matter (*GA* 766^a18–22) and there is produced a female or deficient offspring (*GA* 767^b23). Furthermore, when the semen is defeated in attempting to impose the male form on the female matter, it is

also normally defeated in trying to impose the features of the father
(*GA* 768^{a}25–8), so that on such occasions there occurs a kind of
double defeat or failure.

With such physiological explanations of female inferiority the
Politics shows little concern. It does recognise a connection between
parental age and female offspring (1335^{a}12–15), but does not develop
this point. Its primary concern is with the role of women in society.
The *Politics* is quite clear that men are by nature better than women
(1254^{b}13–14), that men are by nature better fitted to command than
women (1259^{b}2) and that the virtues of men and women are different
(1260^{a}20–4). However, the *Politics* is anxious not to reduce women
to slaves. It states that women are naturally different from slaves
(1252^{a}34–^{b}1) and that among the barbarians women hold the same
position as slaves, only because the barbarians lack a class of natural
rulers, so that the relationship of man and wife comes to be one of
slave and slave (1252^{b}5–7). Focusing upon the household and the
several members of this primary association, and influenced directly
or indirectly by Plato's *Meno*, the *Politics* make clear that the role
of a woman within the household is not the bodily service characteristic of a slave but rather the preservation of goods procured by a
man (1277^{b}24–5; cf. *Oec.* 1344^{a}2–3, *Meno* 71^{e}7). And since virtue
is related to function (1260^{a}16–17, cf. *Meno* 72^{a}2–5), the virtue
demanded of a woman may be expected to reflect her role within the
household. She will need less courage than a man (1277^{b}20–2) and
not the courage of command but rather the courage of subordina-
tion (1260^{a}23; cf. *Meno* 71^{e}7). Similarly she must be temperate
but not in the manner of a man (1260^{a}21). For were a woman
modest in the way that a good man is, she would be a chatterer
(1277^{b}23).

So far Aristotle's account of women is based on his conception
of woman's role within the household. But this is not the end of the
matter. Aristotle also relates women to the distinction between the
logical and alogical halves of the soul (1260^{a}6–7) and contrasts
women with both slaves and children. Slaves are said to possess the
deliberative faculty not at all; women are said to possess it, but
akuron; and children are said to possess it incompletely (1260^{a}12–14).
What Aristotle means in regard to slaves and children has already
been discussed in preceding sections. The case of women is more
obscure. At first glance it may seem that Aristotle is referring to the
subordinate role of women (1259^{b}2, 1260^{a}23). A woman has reason,

but it does not prevail in the society of men. We may think of Tecmessa as depicted in Sophocles' *Ajax*. The intelligence of this woman is never in doubt. She exhibits her cleverness by removing Eurysaces from danger and is accordingly praised for her fore-thought (536). But when she reasons with Ajax and tries to dissuade him from suicide, her words are ineffective. However praiseworthy her arguments, Ajax expects obedience (527–8, cf. 586).[1]

It is, of course, true that a woman's word lacked authority, but this truth does not, I think, do justice to Aristotle's point. In this portion of the *Politics* Aristotle is concerned with the virtues appropriate to different kinds of persons including women. On one level this is not a problem. The *Meno* (72^a2–5) had already suggested that virtue is related to function. Aristotle accepts this principle (1260^a16–17) and applies it to women (1260^a20–4). The problem is on a more fundamental level—namely, why different kinds of people have different functions or roles in society. Here a reference to the new bipartite psychology and to the capacity of deliberation is useful. When Aristotle says that slaves do not possess the delibera-tive capacity, he is not drawing a conclusion based upon the menial role of slaves. Rather he is indicating why slaves have the role they do. They lack the capacity to deliberate, that is to say the ability to act with forethought (1252^a31–2). When this deficiency is com-bined with bodily strength suitable for necessary tasks (1254^b28–9), then the role assigned to slaves by society seems to be a natural role. Similarly in the case of women a reference to their psychological make-up combined with their bodily condition explains their role within the household and therefore ultimately their peculiar kind of virtue. In comparison with man's bodily condition the bodily condition of women is one of weakness, and this comparative weakness points towards a retiring domestic role within the home. Furthermore, their deliberative capacity is *akuron*, that is to say it

---

[1] Tecmessa is perhaps a special case in that she is not only a wife but also a slave captured in battle (Soph., *Ajax* 211, 489). Hence obedience seems especially appropriate. Her case is interesting in that Aristotle's remarks on women do not cover the case of a female slave. In the *Politics* Aristotle focuses on the household and offers an account of woman as wife (1253^b7) in her marriage relationship (1253^b9–11, 1259^a39) to a free man. Presumably Aristotle would say that Tecmessa is by birth (Soph., *Ajax* 487) and also naturally a free woman. Only women lacking deliberative ability are natural slaves and suitable mates for natural male slaves (cf. 1252^b5–7).

lacks authority and is overruled easily.[1] In stating this lack of authority Aristotle is not referring to inter-personal relationships but rather to an intra-personal relationship. Just as he looks within the slave to explain his social position, so he looks within the woman to explain her role and virtues. Her deliberative capacity lacks authority, because it is often overruled by her emotions or alogical side. Her decisions and actions are too often guided by pleasures and pains, so that she is unfitted for leadership and very much in need of temperance.

In calling the deliberative capacity of a woman *akuron*, Aristotle is not impugning the cleverness of women. He recognises that women can think things through and even give reasoned advice. He would see no absurdity, for example, in Ajax praising the forethought of Tecmessa (Soph., *Ajax* 536) or Creon fearing the cleverness of Medea (Eur., *Med.* 285). His point is not that women deliberate only in some vague and illogical way, but that their deliberations and reflections are likely not to control their emotions. This view is, of course, not an Aristotelian creation *ex nihilo*. It is a common view of women and one that is illustrated often in Greek literature. Medea is a celebrated case. Deserted by Jason for another woman, she is angered and plans to take revenge by killing the children born to her and Jason. Reflection tells Medea that such an act of revenge is excessive and against her own interests. She hesitates, but ultimately her *thymos* is stronger than her *bouleumata* (Eur., *Med.* 1079). In other words her *bouleutikon* is *akuron*, so that she acts emotionally and unreasonably, but not without considerable cleverness. Women are most clever contrivers of every evil (Eur., *Med.* 409). In the service of emotion their deliberative faculties are most effective at discovering means to achieve a desired goal. But in controlling and altering unreasonable desires, their deliberative faculties lack authority. Medea understands that she is about to do something terrible (Eur., *Med.* 1078), but she is not deterred by

[1] Newman, *The Politics* 2.218 (following Bonitz, *Index* 29ᵇ61–30ᵃ3), aptly compares the usage of *akuron* at 1260ᵃ13 with *EN* 1151ᵇ15 and translates 'imperfect in authority', 'imperfectly obeyed'. He notes correctly that 'in women *to bouleutikon* is there, but often does not get its own way'. E. Barker, *The Politics of Aristotle* (New York 1962) 35, translates *akuron* rather vaguely with 'inconclusive'. E. Schütrumpf, *Die Bedeutung des Wortes ethos in der Poetik des Aristoteles* (München 1970) 5,54, is not much more precise. He tells us that the deliberative capacity of women is 'unvollkommen', while that of children is 'unfertig'.

this understanding. For in the case of Medea and other women reasoned consideration tends to be *akuron*.[1]

Aristotle's view of women may be false. Certainly the exceptional behaviour of a tragic heroine cannot be said to decide what is in the end an empirical issue. But it would be a mistake to think that Aristotle's view is simply the foolish product of masculine prejudice. On the contrary, it is a thoughtful view that well illustrates the way in which an advance in philosophical psychology can determine developments in political theory.[2] Together with other members of the Academy Aristotle had investigated emotional response and drawn a fundamental distinction between reason and emotion. Aristotle applied this distinction to the field of political theory, formulated a bipartite psychology, and used this psychology to explain the role of women within the city-state. He argued that women have the capacity to reason and therefore are to be distinguished clearly from natural slaves who lack this capacity and from children who have not yet acquired it. Aristotle recognised that women merit a role that is neither servile nor puerile, but he was prepared nevertheless to assign them a subordinate role on the grounds that their reason or logical side is *akuron* in relation to their emotional or alogical side.

---

[1] For a more detailed discussion of Euripides' *Medea* in relation to Aristotle's political and ethical dichotomy, see my 'On the Antecedents', 233-41.

[2] This is not to say that Aristotle's view of women is altogether free of prejudice. It certainly supports the preconceptions of Greek men (including Aristotle) and may serve as a sobering example of how a commendable advance in one area of philosophical concern sometimes finds unfortunate application in another. But admitting all of this, we can still say that Aristotle's view is at least a considered view which does not ignore Plato's insistence that a difference in role be supported by a relevant difference in nature (*Rep.* 454^{c}7-455^{a}3).

CHAPTER FOUR

Consequences for Ethical Theory

1. *A new conception of human virtue*

The Academic investigation of emotion led not only to a new political and ethical psychology but also to a new and more satisfactory conception of moral virtue as a perfection of man's alogical side. Courage was referred to the emotion of fear and good temper to the emotion of anger. The several moral virtues were marked off from one another and at the same time distinguished from forms of knowledge belonging to man's logical side. This is, of course, not an altogether new observation. The author of the *Magna Moralia* asks what is virtue (1182^a8), faults Pythagoras for referring virtue to number (1182^a11-14) and then considers Socrates who is criticised for having made virtues into *epistêmai* and having thereby done away with the alogical half of the soul, emotion and moral character (1182^a15-23). This criticism is of some importance for us, because it recognises an intimate connection between the alogical half of the soul and emotional response and fits well with the claim that the notion of moral virtue advanced in Aristotle's ethical writings was not developed before Plato wrote the *Philebus* and members of the Academy devoted their efforts to working out a clear conception of emotional response. Whether it is Aristotle's first ethical treatise or, as seems more likely, a later work by some Peripatetic follower, the *Magna Moralia* knows the importance of emotional response for elucidating the nature of moral virtue (1186^a33, 1190^b7) and correctly connects Socrates' difficulties in analysing moral virtue with his indifference to emotion and concentration upon *epistêmê*.

This point may be developed by reference to the *Laches* which belongs among Plato's early Socratic dialogues. Here we find Socrates joining with Laches and Nicias in an abortive attempt to state the definition of courage. Nicias recalls hearing Socrates say that a man is good at those things in which he is wise (194^d1-2) and suggests that courage is *epistêmê* or knowledge of what is to be dreaded and to be dared (194ᵉ11–195ᵃ1).[1] This definition survives criticism until Socrates explains the dreadful as that which inspires fear (198ᵇ5) and then defines fear as an expectation of future evil (198ᵇ8–9). He gets Nicias to admit that courage is a knowledge of future evils and goods (198ᶜ2–8) and then using medicine, farming and military science as examples argues that knowledge is never restricted to the future but rather concerns the present and past as well as the future (198ᵈ1–199ᵃ8). Since courage has been agreed to be a knowledge of what is to be dreaded and dared, that is to say a knowledge of future evils and goods, it seems that courage as a form of knowledge must concern itself with present and past as well as future evils and goods (199ᵃ10–ᵈ3). Nicias agrees to this and finds himself with such a magnificent concept of courage that this particular virtue seems to become all virtue and therefore no longer distinct from other virtues like temperance, justice and piety (199ᵈ4–ᵉ4).

The striking feature of this argument is the way in which Socrates treats courage analogously to *epistêmai* like medicine, farming and military science (198ᵈ6, ᵉ1, 3) and extends the sphere of courage from what is to be dreaded and to be dared to all things good and evil (199ᶜ7, ᵈ5). This extension is odd and might have been avoided had Socrates focused on the emotion of fear (198ᵇ6–9) and not gone on to an unfortunate analogy with various *epistêmai*.[2] But Socrates did not focus upon fear and in general ignored emotional response in a way that was typical of his period.[3] It was only later during Aristotle's residence in the Academy that emotions were focused upon. Fear was investigated and shown to be concerned with a limited range of evils—namely, those imminent evils which threaten great pains or destruction (*Rhet.* 1382ᵃ21–5). Once a clear and delimited notion of fear was developed, it was possible to mark off courage from other virtues by relating it to the particular emotion of

---

[1] I agree with G. Santas ('Socrates at Work on Virtue and Knowledge in Plato's *Laches*', *Review of Metaphysics* 22 [1969] 449, note 10, 455) that although in the *Laches* this definition of courage is put in the mouth of Nicias, it is in fact Socrates' own definition that is under scrutiny. Cf. *MM* 1190ᵇ28–32.

[2] On stretching the notion of things to be dreaded and things to be dared and on the comparison with *epistêmai* see Santas, 'Socrates' 456–8, 459.

[3] Even rhetoricians like Thrasymachus and Gorgias, who recognised the power of emotional appeals, spoke only of charms and enchantments (Plato, *Phaedrus* 267ᶜ7–ᵈ1; Gorgias, *Helen* 10, 14) and did not investigate the nature of emotional response. See above, Chapter I, Section 3.

fear. But this development came after Socrates, and the *Magna Moralia* is historically accurate when it connects Socrates' failure to elucidate moral virtue with a general disregard of emotional response and the alogical half of the bipartite soul.

So long as the moral virtues were regarded as *epistêmai*, they could be withheld from animals on the grounds that animals do not engage in those deliberations and reflections that are exercises of *epistêmai*. Hence it is not surprising that in the *Laches* Nicias rejects the idea of courageous animals. First he refuses to call any animal courageous which is fearless on account of thoughtlessness (197ᵃ6–8) and then he adds that courage and forethought belong to very few individuals, while rashness and boldness and fearlessness together with a lack of forethought belong to many men, women, children and animals (197ᵇ2–6). To withhold courage on the grounds that animals are thoughtless may be to say that animals are altogether without cognitive capacity and therefore incapable of making the assessments appropriate to courageous behaviour. But to withhold courage on the grounds that animals lack forethought, while allowing them rashness and boldness, may be to grant animals sanguine expectations and feelings of confidence and to deny them courage only on the grounds that they lack the forethought character-istic of *epistêmai* such as medicine, farming and military science (198ᵈ6, ᵉ1, 3).[1] The latter position seems closer to Nicias' and (we may suppose) Socrates' view. For us the important point is that this position has the consequence that should courage or some form of courage become dissociated from *epistêmê*, the aggressive behaviour of animals could be considered paradigmatic of courageous behaviour. This is clear enough in the *Republic* where Plato dis-tinguishes between the courage of guardians based upon full knowledge and the so-called political courage of auxiliaries (430ᶜ3). Political courage is associated not with knowledge but with true opinion concerning dangers (430ᵇ3). To be sure, Plato does draw a distinction between political courage and bestial and slavish courage on the grounds that the former is and the latter is not the product of

[1] Rashness or recklessness (*thrasytês* 197ᵇ3–4; cf. ᵉ1) may be connected closely with the emotion of feeling confident and with sanguine thoughts about the future. See, for example, Plato's *Laws* where being rash is connected with feeling confident (649ᶜ8–9, cf. Arist. *EN* 1115ᵇ28) and confidence is said to be a kind of expectation (*elpis*) or opinion (*doxa*) about the future (644ᶜ9–ᵈ1, 649ᵃ4–ᵇ3, cf. *EN* 1116ᵃ4, *Rhet.* 1383ᵃ18).

an educational system (430^{b}7). But Plato does not explicitly dissociate animals from true opinion concerning dangers[1] and therefore leaves open the possibility that the courage of animals may be cognitive and differ from political courage only in so far as it is not the product of musical and gymnastic education (430^{a}1). Moreover, when Plato considers the nature appropriate to auxiliaries and guardians, he connects courage with being spirited (375^{a}11), introduces the well-bred hound as a model (375^{d}5) and suggests that there is no significant difference between the spirited nature of such a hound and the virtuous character of a noble youth (375^{a}2–3). This tendency to equate the temperament of animals with the moral character of human beings is intelligible enough. Members of the Academy had not as yet focused upon emotion and therefore had not developed a clear idea of cognitive responses peculiar to human beings. It was only later when Aristotle pinned down the

---

[1] It is tempting to say that Glaucon's remark about a bestial and slavish right opinion not arising through education (430^{b}6–9) actually attributes opinion to animals. Certainly, if we take Glaucon's remark rather literally and hold that he recognises some kind of right opinion appropriate to animals (cf. J. Adam, *The Republic of Plato*, 2nd ed. [Cambridge 1963] 1.231 who defends the text against those who would alter it on the grounds that animals cannot have right opinion) and if we interpret this passage by reference to remarks in the second book concerning the natural temperament of guardians (374^{e}6–376^{e}6) and hold that Glaucon wants to mark off natural temperament from the courage of a citizen (cf. Görgemanns, *Beiträge* 125), then it would seem that the natural temperament requisite for courage is in part at least cognitive and that animals share in this temperament because they share in opinion. This interpretation is possible, but weakly supported by the text. The idea of a nature suitable for courage does occur in this portion of the *Republic* (429^{d}5–6, ^{e}8, 430^{a}4). But Glaucon does not say that he is marking off this natural temperament from political courage, and in the absence of such a statement there seems to be no compelling reason for interpreting Glaucon's words this way. Furthermore, to call an opinion bestial is not necessarily to say that animals hold such opinions. Hence the addition of 'slavish' (430^{b}8), which has a similar use at *Phaedo* 69^{b}7. The simplest explanation is, I think, the best. Glaucon recognises that a man can hold a right opinion concerning danger even though he has not been through a formal system of moral education. Such an opinion may be right but it is likely not to be action-guiding during moments of crisis. It will, so to speak, fade in the manner of dye that has been applied without proper preparation (429^{e}3–5). When Socrates defines courage without a reference to education, Glaucon adds for the sake of clarity that Socrates does not mean by courage a right opinion arising apart from education (430^{b}7). His remark is simply a negative restatement of 429^{e}7, 430^{a}1–3 and has nothing to do with animals and their cognitive capacity. 'Bestial' is used as a pejorative label and nothing more.

cognitive nature of emotion, refused animals a share in cognition and tied moral virtue to emotional response that animal temperament was decisively marked off from human virtue. Animals could be seen to lack courage and other moral virtues not because they lack forethought typical of *epistêmai* or happen to miss out on musical and gymnastic education, but rather because they lack thought altogether and therefore cannot respond emotionally in the way human beings do.

This is such an important point that it is worth spelling out in some detail. Aristotle's position is that while animals possess *aisthêsis* (1139^{a}20, 1170^{a}16) and therefore experience pleasant and painful sensations and utter sounds as signs of such sensations, they lack the human capacity to distinguish between good and evil, justice and injustice and to communicate such judgments through speech (*Pol.* 1253^{a}10–18). Only human beings have the capacity to think (*De An.* 414^{b}18–19, 415^{a}7–9, 427^{b}6–14), so that animals cannot hold a *doxa* or opinion (*De An.* 427^{b}8–14, 428^{a}18–24, 434^{a}5–11).[1] This means that animals cannot act upon an opinion

---

[1] I do not wish to suggest that the *Corpus Aristotelicum* is without ambiguities in regard to animals. (For a fuller discussion of animals and especially of passages which seem to count against the view advanced in this section see my 'Aristotle: Animals', 137–65.) But I do wish to insist that the major thrust of Aristotle's own biological thought is towards a rigid *scala naturae* which fixes animals at the level of *aisthêsis*. Moreover, I think recent scholars have erred in saying that *De An.* 434^{a}10–11 and *De Mem.* 450^{a}15–16 attribute *doxa* to animals. The first of these passages I have discussed already in my 'Aristotle: Animals', 158–9. Here I would only repeat that these lines concern imagination and not animals which were last mentioned back in 434^{a}6. The second passage I have not discussed and therefore wish to comment upon a bit more fully. It seems to me a mistake to interpret this passage in such a way that Aristotle is made to mention or refer to 'animals that have judgment or intelligence' (R. Sorabji, *Aristotle on Memory* [London 1972] 49; cf. 77–8). Hett (in the Loeb edition, 293) was on the right track when he translated 'men and beings which are capable of opinion and thought'. In 450^{a}16 Aristotle is not saying that some animals (the word 'animals' does not occur in the text) possess *doxa* and *phronêsis*. Rather he is adding a phrase which indicates what it is to have intellect (the *kai* in 450^{a}16 may be epexegetical) and at the same time seems to allow the possibility of other thinking beings besides men. We may compare *De An.* 414^{b}18–19 where Aristotle attributes *to dianoêtikon* and *nous* to men and to any other beings there may be which are like or more honourable than men. In this passage from the *De Anima* Aristotle is not suddenly elevating the psychic powers of certain animals but rather recognising that thinking may not be peculiar to men. (It is only peculiar to men when qualified by 'in relation to animals'; cf. *Pol.* 1253^{a}16.)

and cannot respond emotionally to a particular situation. For an emotion such as fear involves opining or thinking (*doxazein*, *De An.* 427ᵇ21) something terrible. It is an expectation (*prosdokia*, *EN* 1115ᵃ9, *Rhet.* 1382ᵇ29; cf. Plato, *Laches* 198ᵇ9, *Prot.* 358ᵈ6, *Laws* 646ᵉ7–8) of imminent evil and therefore impossible for creatures lacking intellect and reacting only in accordance with pleasant and painful *aisthêsis*. Of course, the reactions of animals are not entirely passive. They involve discrimination and therefore may be said to manifest critical capacity. Aristotle is not unaware of this. He connects *aisthêsis* with *krisis* (*De An.* 418ᵃ14, 426ᵇ10, 427ᵃ20, 432ᵃ16)[1] and recognises the importance of sensory discrimination for the survival and well-being of animals (*De An.* 434ᵇ9–435ᵇ25). When he is concerned with locomotion, he does not hesitate to group together *aisthêsis* and *nous* as critical faculties distinct from the faculty of locomotion (*MA* 700ᵇ19–22; cf. *De An.* 432ᵃ16–17). And when he is thinking of animals in comparison with plants and of *aisthêsis* in comparison with insensibility, he is prepared to speak of *aisthêsis* as a kind of knowing (*gnôsis tis*) which is very fine and preferable to the non-existence of death (*GA* 731ᵃ30–ᵇ4). But Aristotle would certainly object to an unqualified identification of animal discrimination with human judgment. He would insist that only the latter can be a *doxa* open to persuasive *logos* (*De An.*

[1] For additional references see D. W. Hamlyn, 'Aristotle's Account of Aesthesis in the *De Anima*', *Classical Quarterly* 9 (1959) 8.

There are gods and perhaps other beings which are like men in possessing thought. Similarly in the *De Memoria* Aristotle does not violate his *scala naturae*. He simply adds a phrase which seems to allow for but does not explicitly name certain non-human (not sub-human) beings possessing *doxa* and *phronêsis*. I express myself cautiously, because the *kai* might be considered epexegetical and therefore the entire phrase might be considered simply explanatory of human capacity. But I am inclined to say that Aristotle's wording suggests the possibility of other thinking beings beside men. For Aristotle goes on to speak of mortal creatures and to argue that were memory one of the thinking parts, it might not belong to any mortal being (450ᵃ16–19). If we understand the preceding mention of beings possessing *doxa* and *phronêsis* in such a way that it makes room for, or suggests, immortal thinkers, then we should not be surprised that Aristotle goes on to develop a mortal-immortal contrast (cf. Sorabji 79) and certainly should not wish to follow Förster and Ross in altering *thnêtôn* to *anoetôn* (450ᵃ18). Of course, none of this commits Aristotle to the view that God has memory (on this Sorabji [79] is correct), but it also does nothing to dignify certain animals by attributing *doxa* to them.

428^{a}22–4).[1] Animal pursuit can be called a *quasi*-affirmation and animal flight can be called a *quasi*-denial (*De An.* 431^{a}9–10). But for Aristotle animal behaviour remains only analogous to the judgments and emotional responses of human beings. It is governed by pleasant and painful *aisthêsis* and does not qualify as action (*praxis* 1139^{a}20).

It follows that animals cannot possess moral virtue, for moral virtue is concerned with emotions and actions (1104^{b}13–14, 1106^{b}24–5, 1109^{b}30). It is a *hexis* whereby men are well-disposed with regard to emotional response (1105^{b}19–1106^{a}13) and therefore is a peculiarly human virtue (1102^{a}14, 16, ^{b}3, 12). Courage is no exception. Aristotle is quite clear that courage is a cognitive disposition characteristic of men who have learned to despise (*kataphronein* 1104^{b}1) danger, that is to say of men who have learned to think danger of little or no importance (cf. *Rhet.* 1378^{b}16–17) and to express this negative assessment in action by steadfast endurance. Moreover, courageous men endure fearsome situations because it is noble to do so (1115^{b}12, 23, 1116^{a}11, ^{b}31). They not only respond to danger with endurance but also see their responses in a certain way—namely, as instances of noble action. Courage, therefore, is a human disposition not found in animals lacking cognitive capacity. Aristotle does not miss this point and says explicitly that the dispositions of animals differ in kind from the virtues and vices of human beings (1145^{a}25–7), so that animals are called temperate and intemperate only in a metaphorical sense (1149^{b}31–2). Virtue may be said to make a horse good at facing the enemy (1106^{a}19–21), but this virtuous disposition is not to be confused with the courage of human beings. Horses live by sensation

---

[1] Aristotle would never deny that the discriminations of animals may be quite remarkable. He knew his Homer and would be familiar with the story of how the dying dog Argos marked the presence of Odysseus after an absence of twenty years (*Od.* 17.290–327). Moreover, Aristotle would not fault Homer for using the verb *noein* (17.301) to describe this incredible case of perceptivity. But he would say that Argos' perception does not involve opining and that canine discriminations in general are not to be confused with acts of thinking peculiar to creatures possessing *logos* (*De An.* 427^{b}8–14). For being a thinking, cognitive creature involves being open to reasoned persuasion in a way that no dog ever is. Of course, dogs may be obedient, but their obedience does not depend upon opinions and convictions which are in principle at least open to the persuasion of reasoned *logos* (*De An.* 428^{a}18–24; cf. *EN* 1098^{a}1–5, 1102^{b}31–1103^{a}3, discussed above, Chapter Two, Section 2, and *Pol.* 1254^{b}22–4, discussed above, Chapter Three, Section 3).

(1098^a2), while human beings have intellect. Only men have an alogical half that can be perfected by moral virtue.[1]

2. *Virtuous action without calculation*

In our previous discussion of young people and moral education (Chapter Three, Sections 1 and 2) we observed how the Academic investigation of emotional response led not only to a new political and ethical psychology but also to a new formulation of educational theory. Moral *paideia* was referred to the alogical half of the soul and recognised as a training in values occurring before the development and education of man's logical side. An important consequence was that Aristotle could recognise the value of a virtuous disposition quite apart from deliberation and practical wisdom. This is most obvious in regard to younger persons who are said to live more by *êthos* than by the calculations of *logismos* (*Rhet.* 1389^a33–4). They lack the deliberative excellence that is practical wisdom (*phronêsis*), so that their good behaviour is a matter of virtuous character directed towards the noble (*Rhet.* 1389^a35). Of course, Aristotle would not say that younger people have moral virtue in the strict sense implying the presence of practical wisdom (*EN* 1144^b16–17). In the best of circumstances the character of younger persons derives from an education under law (*Rhet.* 1389^a29) and therefore ultimately depends upon the practical wisdom of a legislator. But it remains true that younger people can acquire moral principles and an established disposition to act in accordance with these principles. In other words they can acquire through *paideia* a virtuous *êthos* of real practical significance. Moreover, mature men who have acquired not only a virtuous *êthos* but also practical wisdom may find themselves in situations where their practical wisdom is of no use. Like young people, they simply respond correctly without

---

[1] In regard to animal behaviour and virtue it is worth mentioning that the account of Peripatetic doctrine given in the fifth book of Cicero's *De Finibus* presents substantially the same view. Sense faculties are distinguished from intellect to which are referred all virtues (5.34) including both those called *non voluntariae* and those that are *in voluntate positae*—namely, prudence, temperance, courage and justice. In other words, not only the intellectual virtue of prudence but also the several moral virtues are dissociated from sensation and associated with intellect. Since animals are marked by sensation and not intellect (5.40), they cannot possess virtue, though lions, dogs and horses may possess *aliquid simile virtutis* (5.38).

reflecting upon various possible courses of action. Their good behaviour is a matter of moral virtue and not of practical wisdom.

This will become clearer if we consider the case of the more courageous man (1117ª18). Men with good expectations (*euelpides*) are, according to Aristotle, similar to but not the same as courageous men. They endure because they think themselves superior in strength and immune to harm, but they flee when events run counter to their expectations. In contrast, a courageous man may be expected to endure real and apparent dangers, because it is noble to do so and shameful not to do so (1117ª9–17). Having drawn this contrast between the man who endures because he thinks himself secure and the man who endures because endurance is noble, Aristotle argues that it is the mark of a more courageous man to be fearless in sudden alarms rather than in foreseen dangers. For in sudden alarms fearlessness results more from an established disposition than from preparation. When events are foreseen a man may make a choice based upon calculation and reason, but when events occur suddenly a man chooses in accordance with his disposition (1117ª17–22).¹ Sudden alarms do not permit a man to

---

¹ *Proeloito* (1117ª21) is understood in 1117ª22. Hence I prefer the translations of Gauthier and Jolif (*L'Éthique* 1.81) and A. E. Wardman (*The Philosophy of Aristotle* edited by R. Bambrough [New York 1963] 331) to that of Ostwald (*Ethics* 75). Emotional responses can occur without choice, but not those of the virtuous man (1106ª2–4; cf. 1105ᵇ28–33). However, it might be objected that understanding *proeloito* in 1117ª22 commits Aristotle to inconsistency. For choice is explained in terms of deliberation (1112ª15, 1113ª2–12, 1139ª23) and deliberation is said to be a kind of search (1112ᵇ20–3, 1142ª31–2) involving calculation and reasoning (1139ª12–13, 1142ᵇ1–3, 12–15, 19–20). In a sudden situation such as confronts the more courageous man there is no time for calculation and reasoning (1117ª21) and therefore no time for search and deliberation. Hence if we understand *proeloito* and say that the more courageous man chooses, we seem committed to saying that Aristotle breaks the stated connection between choice and deliberation and in so doing involves himself in a certain inconsistency. But if this is inconsistency, it seems to be welcome inconsistency. For if Aristotle maintains both the connection between virtue and choice and also the connection between choice and deliberation, he seems committed to saying that every time a courageous man acts virtuously he engages in deliberation, search and calculation. It is doubtful that Aristotle would want to say this. For not only does it seem implausible to hold that a courageous man always deliberates (searches something out, asks himself questions) before he acts (cf. Sorabji, 'Intellect in Virtue', 112), but also it seems to fit poorly with Aristotle's own remarks on thought and action. For in the *Movement of Animals*, Aristotle is explicit that action need not be preceded by question-asking, that

consider various means of meeting danger. They rule out preparations and good expectations based upon calculated estimations of superiority, and therefore may be expected to expose the true character of persons who endure dangers only because they think themselves superior.

For our purposes the important thing to note is that the more courageous individual chooses to endure because of his moral character and not as a result of calculation (*logismos*) and reason (*logos*). Using the language of Aristotle's newly won political and ethical psychology we may say that in sudden alarms the logical half of the soul does not come into play, because there is not time for reflection and deliberation. Response to sudden danger depends entirely on the alogical half of the bipartite soul, and if this half has been trained properly the response will be appropriate to the situation. Having been taught that endurance is noble and having been habituated to despise things that are fearsome, a courageous individual can be counted upon to meet sudden dangers by choosing endurance because it is noble and shameful not to do so ($1117^{a}17$). In contrast, a coward can be counted on to choose safety in flight. He has not been taught to despise danger and to value endurance. His choice manifests an ignorance attributable to moral character alone ($1110^{b}31-2$).

Aristotle's example of sudden danger is of especial interest in that it seems to use vocabulary reminiscent of Plato's *Laches*[1] and to help unravel the dilemma created when Socrates suggests that courage is endurance with wisdom ($192^{c}8$, $^{d}10$) and then goes on to argue that the soldier who fights willingly after calculating wisely his

---

[1] For these reminiscences, see my 'Aristotle: Animals' 161, note 25.

---

we do not stop to consider the obvious and that whatever we do without calculating, we do quickly ($701^{a}25-9$; cf. *EN* $1112^{a}34-^{b}8$, $34-1113^{a}2$). The application of these remarks to the more courageous man seems straightforward. He is disposed by moral training to endure danger for the sake of the noble. Confronted by sudden alarms he sees his situation as an occasion for noble endurance. Instead of pausing to deliberate, he chooses straightway to lay his life on the line. Assuming that Aristotle does not want to break the connection between virtue and choice (and I do not think he does), he does well to break the connection between choice and deliberation, for there are situations such as sudden alarms where it is both implausible psychology to maintain that a man pauses to ask himself questions (cf. *MA* $701^{a}31$) and also bad ethics to suggest that he ought to do so. The mark of superior virtue is often immediate response. Delay and questioning are frequently signs of inferior moral character.

own superiority, would not be called more courageous than his opponent who endures willingly despite a position of inferiority (193ᵃ3–9). After securing agreement on this point, Socrates suggests that the endurance of the disadvantaged soldier is less wise than that of the superior soldier (193ᵇ2–3) and then presses the argument to the unhappy conclusion that courage is unwise endurance and therefore something shameful and not noble (193ᵈ1–7). This is certainly an unfortunate conclusion and one which is to be avoided by rejecting the alternatives set up by Socrates. Willing endurance following upon calculations of advantage is no paradigm of courageous behaviour. But neither is the foolish endurance of a man lacking in advantage. We need a third case in which courageous behaviour is removed from calculations and yet not reduced to the rash endurance of an incompetent fool. Aristotle's example of the more courageous man provides just such a case. With calculations of advantage excluded by the suddenness of the situation, emotional response alone is possible, and this is either virtuous or not depending upon the moral character of the agent. The more courageous man assesses the situation correctly and responds courageously, though he has not had time to engage in calculations which belong to the logical half of the soul and fall within the province of practical wisdom.

We can say, then, that Aristotle's concern with emotional response helped him to resolve a Socratic puzzle and to develop a conception of moral virtue which recognises the importance of virtuous action apart from calculation. Moral virtue became a stochastic (1106ᵇ15–16, 28, 1109ᵃ22, 30) disposition whereby a man is able to aim at and hit upon the mean between excessive and deficient emotional response (1106ᵇ15–18). Hitting upon the mean is a critical act and therefore properly referred to a cognitive per-fection. But as Aristotle saw, such a critical act need not be assigned to practical wisdom. At times of emotional response there need be no deliberation or reflection, that is to say no logical activity. The entire response may be referred to the alogical half of the soul and its stochastic perfection. Indeed the label *stochastikē* suggests this, for *eustochia* is said to be something quick and without *logos* (1142ᵇ2–3).[1] In sudden situations men do not choose as a result of

[1] This is not to say that Aristotle never uses the label *stochastikos* to describe a good deliberator. He does (1141ᵇ13–14), but as a metaphor from archery (cf. Plato, *Laws* 706ᵃ1) it need not imply deliberation and seems to be used more aptly to describe cases where deliberation is minimal or altogether absent.

logismos and *logos* (1117ᵃ21). They must respond quickly, hitting upon a mean or proper mode of action without the benefit of reflection and deliberation.[1]

The foregoing is not contradicted by repeated assertions to the effect that the mean is determined by right reason and practical wisdom (1103ᵇ31-4, 1106ᵇ36-1107ᵃ2, 1114ᵇ26-30, 1138ᵇ18-25). These assertions only commit Aristotle to the view that questions concerning what counts as virtuous behaviour are ultimately decided by reasoning. They do not commit Aristotle to the view that the particular acts of a virtuous person are always to be explained by reference to the activity of practical wisdom. Aristotle never says (and in my opinion never wants to say) that every time a virtuous man makes a correct moral perception and acts virtuously, his practical wisdom is in play. The reason he does not make this claim is that he works with a distinction between two fundamental modes of human behaviour: emotional response and reasoned reflection, and correlates this distinction with an ethical distinction between moral virtue and practical wisdom. Of course, when a man reflects about his own or someone else's behaviour, then questions concerning the mean are decided by reasoning. And for understanding Aristotle's ethical thought it is a point of some importance that Aristotle recognises the authority of reasoned argumentation. Assertions concerning the mean and evaluations in general become authoritative when they are explained and justified. But to say this is not to say that every exercise of moral virtue necessarily involves an exercise of practical wisdom. Aristotle holds only that moral virtue in the strict sense is with (*meta* 1144ᵇ27) practical wisdom. That is, the perfect man of total virtue has both moral virtue and

---

[1] A clarification may be helpful. I do not want to say that all kinds of un-reflective judgments are to be assigned to the alogical half of the soul. That would be just as much a mistake as attributing all such judgments to the logical half. In the course of deliberations when emotions are not in play, a man may have an insight and hit upon something in advance of his deliberations. Or to take an example from the *Rhetoric*, while doing philosophy a man may perceive similarities between things far apart and show himself to be *eustochos* like Archytas, who said that an arbitrator and an altar were the same, for at both an injured person finds refuge (1412ᵃ12-15). (Cf. Plato, *Laws* 792ᵈ3 and 950ᵇ8 with Gauthier and Jolif, *L'Éthique* 2.511.) During periods of deliberation and philosophic reflection, insight is not part of an emotional response and is not to be referred to the alogical half of the soul. But in moments of emotional response, hitting upon the mean belongs to the alogical half and the perfected disposition of moral virtue.

practical wisdom. He has not only been through an early system of *paideia* and thereby acquired good principles and proper loves and hates. He has also learned to reflect both about a particular course of behaviour and about general principles. But such total perfection does not rule out exercising moral virtue apart from practical wisdom. It is compatible with non-reflective emotional response.

3. *Moral virtue and the goal of action*

Towards the end of the sixth book of the *Ethics* Aristotle raises the question whether practical wisdom is necessary. He recognises that practical wisdom is concerned with what is just, noble and good, but queries whether practical wisdom is useful in enhancing the ability of a virtuous man to do what is morally right (1143^b18–36). In answer to this question Aristotle says that practical wisdom is a virtue and so desirable in itself, even if it does not produce anything. Furthermore, practical wisdom does contribute to proper performance. For while moral virtue makes the goal correct, practical wisdom makes the means correct (1144^a1–9). This answer is a difficulty for anyone who does not understand Aristotle's conception of emotion and therefore confuses Aristotle's political and ethical dichotomy with his biological distinction between sensation and intelligence. Were the emotional or alogical half of the bipartite soul divorced from cognition and identical with the biological faculty of sensation, Aristotle might be expected to point out that a perfection of the alogical half is never sufficient to ensure morally good behaviour, for such behaviour involves judgment and assessment which are cognitive acts properly attributed to the biological faculty of intelligence. But Aristotle does not offer this reply, because it is based upon an erroneous interpretation of his political and ethical psychology. Instead he tells us that moral virtue makes the end correct and practical wisdom the means to the end (1144^a7–9). His point is quite simple and straightforward. As a perfection of man's emotional side, moral virtue makes correct the judgments and goals involved in emotional response.[1] A courageous man, for

---

[1] I cannot agree with Allan (*The Philosophy* 182) who argues that Aristotle 'is careful *not* to say that moral virtue can furnish us with a true *judgment* about the good or end which ought to be pursued; it cannot do this, because it is not a state of mind but an emotional disposition whereby pleasure and pain are rightly felt.' In arguing this way Allan is confusing emotion as an element in

example, becomes frightened and desires safety only when it is right to do so. When the situation calls for endurance, he perceives this and responds boldly because it is noble to do so. All this falls within the province of moral virtue.[1] What moral virtue does not make correct is the means-end deliberation occasioned by emotional response. Fear, as Aristotle says, makes men deliberators (*Rhet.* 1383ᵃ6–7). When they become frightened, men desire safety and therefore engage in deliberations about how to secure safety. Moral virtue makes the goal correct, but it cannot make the deliberations correct. Means-end deliberations are exercises of the logical half of the soul and fall within the province of practical wisdom.

Still concerned with whether or not practical wisdom increases a man's ability to do what is just and noble, Aristotle points out that a good man chooses his actions for their own sake and that choice is made correct by moral virtue. It is, however, not virtue but rather another capacity that is said to determine the steps naturally taken for the sake of choice. Aristotle notes that men call this capacity cleverness (*deinotês*) and adds that it is praiseworthy if the goal is

[1] In responding to a particular danger a courageous man may be influenced by many different beliefs and desires. Having been through a comprehensive system of *paideia* he will have learned not only to value endurance in the face of death but also to desire honour and the leisure which results from resisting aggression. Furthermore, if he is a mature man of practical wisdom, he will have reflected upon his several goals and come to a reasoned understanding of how they relate to one another. This means that a courageous response may be made against a quite complicated background of goals and values. But to say this is not to say that every time a courageous man chooses to endure danger, he reflects upon his various goals and values. He may simply choose endurance without any reflection or deliberation at all (see above, Section 2, with n.1 pp. 71–2). In such a case his choice is an emotional response free from any active exercise of practical wisdom. Its correctness is attributable entirely to moral virtue.

---

bipartition with sensation and motive force as elements in the biological psychology. So is Monan (*Moral Knowledge* 78–9) when he argues that Aristotle never turns over the determination of the goal to 'blind desire' and that 'all those texts which seemingly attribute the setting of goals to moral virtue in fact only stress the need of both *phronêsis* and moral virtue in the process'. Once we understand that the alogical half of the bipartite soul is not to be identified with blind desires, we will not feel compelled to search for a sophisticated interpretation of Aristotle's words, but can construe them in a straightforward manner. Cf. P. Aubenque, *La Prudence chez Aristote* (Paris 1963) 118 note 5 and 'La prudence aristotélicienne porte-t-elle sur la fin ou sur les moyens?', *Revue des Études Grecques* 58 (1965), 40–51 replying to the criticisms of Gauthier reviewing *La Prudence* in *Revue des Études Grecques* 56 (1963) 266–7.

noble, but knavery (*panourgia*) if the goal is base. Practical wisdom is said to be not without this capacity of cleverness and also not without virtue. The reason for this is that the syllogisms of practical deliberations begin from principles to the effect that such and such is the goal and the best. Only a morally good man gets these principles correct, for wickedness distorts and makes a man err in regard to principles of action (1144^a11-^b1).

Aristotle's point remains basically the same: moral virtue ensures a correct goal, while practical wisdom as a perfection of man's logical side is responsible for correct means-end deliberations. Only now Aristotle makes even clearer that the moral value of means-end deliberations is determined by the goal they serve. This is hardly a new discovery. In Sophocles' *Antigone* Creon acknowledges the intelligence of Teiresias but assigns him to the class of greedy individuals who are clever (*deinoi*) in using *logoi* for the sake of gain (1045–7, 1055, 1059). According to Creon there is nothing wrong with Teiresias' calculating ability. It is his love of money (1055) which is bad and which infects his *logoi* rendering them shameful, though well stated (1057). With this passage from Greek tragedy we may compare a passage in the *Laws* where the Athenian Stranger points out that mathematical calculations quicken the mind and are fine and appropriate forms of training so long as illiberality and love of money are removed from the soul. For when these vices are not removed the result is knavery (*panourgia*) instead of wisdom (747^b3-^c3). The Stranger, like Creon, recognises how a misguided love of material gain affects the value we place upon deliberative ability. Illiberality and vice in general determine a man's goals and so the value of his means-end deliberations. Aristotle acknowledges this by refusing to identify practical wisdom with mere cleverness (1144^a28-9) and by pointing out that cleverness in conjunction with a base goal is knavery (1144^a27).

Here a caveat may be in order. When Aristotle says that virtue makes choice correct (1144^a20), he does not mean that there is no sense in which practical wisdom can be said to make choice correct. In his discussion of choice in the third book of the *Ethics* Aristotle concerns himself with choosing means (1111^b27) which are certainly the province of practical wisdom. Moreover, at the end of the sixth book when Aristotle summarises his views on the desirability and utility of practical wisdom, he says that choice will not be correct without practical wisdom and virtue, for the latter makes a man do the goal, while the former makes a man do the means leading to the goal (1145^a4–6). Still, the earlier association of choice with moral virtue alone is not a regrettable slip on Aristotle's part. He is defending the usefulness of practical wisdom by reference to its role in means-end deliberations. Since this role is primarily a technical performance without independent moral value, choice *qua* moral choice is referred naturally to moral virtue.[1] It is choosing to do something for its own sake which exhibits moral character (1144^a18–20), not thinking up ways to achieve some goal already chosen as something noble and desirable in its own right. A courageous man, for example, manifests his good character by choosing to endure danger because it is noble to do so, not by a clever selection of means to meet and survive danger. This is why Aristotle recognises that sudden dangers are a better test of moral character than foreseen dangers. When preparations and calculations are excluded, moral character alone determines whether or not a man chooses to endure (1117^a18–22). This is not to say that moral virtue excludes or is in any way hostile to deliberation. In fact, moral virtue is valued partly because it enables a man to deliberate. Courageous men are quick in the midst of action, but calm beforehand (1116^a9). Their fearless disposition enables them 'to keep their cool' and therefore to consider not only how to meet oncoming danger but also whether this particular situation is in fact the kind of situation that demands noble endurance.[2] But when Aristotle is thinking of choice as

[1] I say 'primarily a technical performance', because there are occasions when means-end deliberations involve moral choices. When there are several ways to achieve a goal, men consider which way is easiest and best (1112^b16–17). Clearly the easiest way need not be the best, for it may be morally offensive. In such cases we may select a more difficult way in preference to the easiest. But we do not always do so, for sometimes we think the importance of the end justifies the means.

[2] I agree with Allan (*The Philosophy* 181–2) that in the last chapter of *EN*6 Aristotle is focusing upon a function of practical wisdom which makes clear its practical importance and that Aristotle does not say that practical wisdom has no other function than the selection of means (cf. Gauthier and Jolif, *L'Éthique* 2.565). When a man engages in reasoned reflection concerning the general goals of life or a particular goal in a particular situation, he is using the logical half of the soul and therefore needs practical wisdom. But I cannot follow Allan in concluding that only practical wisdom can provide us with a true judgment of the end (see above, p.75 n.1). Such a conclusion ignores cases when only the alogical half of the soul is in play. At times of emotional response a morally virtuous man may act for a correct goal without any reflection at all or with only means-end deliberations and without consideration of his goal.

moral choice and of practical wisdom in regard to technical deliberations about means, he understandably connects choice with moral
virtue conceived of as an established disposition to assess correctly
the particular situation and to act for noble ends.[1]

4. Practical and non-practical emotions

A thorough investigation of emotional response enabled Aristotle
to understand and explain the cognitive nature of emotional response,
the relation of emotion to reason and the corresponding relation
of moral virtue to practical wisdom. This is not the end of the
matter. Aristotle's investigations of emotional response also made
clear that some emotions are practical and others non-practical
and that the latter class of emotions does not admit moral virtue in
the way that the former class does. Consider, for example, the
moral virtue of courage. This virtue is connected with fear which is
a practical emotion involving safety as a goal. Frightened men are not
aimless. They desire safety and direct their actions towards this
end. In the *Rhetoric* Aristotle makes this quite clear when he tells

[1] It may be noted that the *Eudemian Ethics*, like the *Nicomachean Ethics*, is
explicit concerning the importance of moral virtue for assessing correctly the
particular situation (1230^a31, 1232^a35-6) and for having a proper goal (1227^b23-
24). This is intelligible, for the *Eudemian Ethics* is also explicit that both halves
of the bipartite soul are peculiar to the human soul (1219^b37-8) and that moral
virtue is a human virtue (1219^b27). Apparently moral virtue is not conceived
of as a perfection in regard to the sensations and thrusts common to men and
animals. Its sphere is thought to go beyond such non-cognitive phenomena and
to include the opinions and moral principles taught to young persons as part of
their moral *paideia*. What the early *paideia* does not instil is a reasoned defence
or explanation of such opinions and principles. This is why the *Eudemian
Ethics* says that moral virtue makes the end correct and then explains that this is
not a matter of *logismos* and *logos* (1227^b24-5). The *Eudemian Ethics* is well aware
that many people hold opinions about what ought to be done, even though
these opinions are not the product of *logismos* (1226^b23-5). The morally virtuous
man is but a particular case. He has been habituated to believe that certain kinds
of actions are good and desirable. In other words, he has acquired goals which
are action-guiding. Of course, he may also be able to explain these goals and he
may be able to deliberate about means to achieve these goals. But such explanations and deliberations do not manifest moral virtue. They are exercises of
logismos whose perfection is practical wisdom. The training of moral *paideia* is
not a training in reasoning but rather a practical training in values. The *Eudemian
Ethics* can say without qualification that moral virtue makes correct the goal,
because the morally virtuous man has learned moral principles which determine
the goals of his particular actions.

us that for a man to be frightened there must be some hope of safety, for fear makes men deliberate and no one deliberates concerning things considered hopeless (1383^a5–8). When men become frightened, they think safety possible and in the absence of any restraining influence act for the sake of safety. Their emotion is practical in the sense that it involves a particular kind of goal and normally manifests itself in a particular kind of goal-directed behaviour.

Something similar can be said concerning the emotion of anger which is related by Aristotle to the moral virtue of good temper (1108^a4–6, 1125^b26). Anger is a practical emotion aiming at revenge. Aristotle makes this clear in the *Rhetoric* where he defines anger as a desire for revenge (1378^a30) and states that when revenge appears impossible, anger is absent (1370^b13). Anger, we are told, is accompanied by pleasure arising from the expectation of taking revenge. For it is pleasant to think that one will obtain that at which one aims. No one aims at what appears to be impossible, and the angry man aims at what seems possible to him (1378^b1–4). In other words, being angry is not a matter of idle wishes. The emotion of anger is like the emotion of fear. Both are practical in the sense of involving a possible goal for which one acts.[1] Aristotle recognises

---

[1] It might be objected that our everyday notions of fear and anger do not demand a possible goal. We would not deny on conceptual grounds that a prisoner bound to a post before a row of archers with bows drawn taut may be frightened of death and angry at those who informed against him. Three points should be made. First, there is no reason why Aristotle's conception of fear and anger must be exactly like our own. It may differ and differ in a way that helps us understand Aristotle's repeated assertions that moral virtue (conceived of as a practical disposition 1104^b28) concerns emotion and action (*EN* 1104^b13–14, 1106^b16–17, 1107^a4–5, 1108^b18–19, 1109^a23, $^b30$). In making this assertion, Aristotle is not thinking of emotion and action as two totally distinct phenomena. Rather he is thinking primarily of practical emotions (e.g., fear and anger) involving goal-directed action. Secondly, Aristotle holds only that the goal must not appear to be impossible (*Rhet.* 1370^b13), that there must be some expectation (1378^b2, 1383^a5) of safety or revenge. He does not deny that a frightened or angry man may on occasion be in a hopeless position and either not realise it or cling to some quite irrational fantasy of safety or revenge. Thirdly, even if Aristotle's analysis of fear and anger involves some departure from our own conception of these emotions, it may exhibit considerable grasp of empirical psychology. For when a condemned prisoner is tied to a post and clearly confronted with the hopelessness of his situation, he sometimes (perhaps often) stops trembling and growling. Realising that death is both certain and imminent, he ceases to be frightened and angry. His practical emotions give way to appropriate, non-practical feelings such as despair and resignation.

the importance of such practical emotions and makes them central to his conception of moral virtue and man's alogical side. He conceives of courageous and good tempered men as 'doers', describes their dispositions as practical and associates them with choice (1104ᵇ28, 1106ᵃ2–4, *Rhet.* 1366ᵇ11). This choice is no idle wish. Aristotle is quite clear that choice is not of the impossible (1111ᵇ20–1) but rather of that which is within a man's power (1111ᵇ30). The dispositions of courage and good temper are perfections of practical emotions and are themselves practical. They are exhibited in goal-directed responses which are justified by the situation and directed towards a noble goal.

If practical emotions are central to Aristotle's conception of the *alogon*, they are not all that belong within this psychic half. Aristotle had thoroughly studied emotional response and was well aware that not every emotion is practical in the way that fear and anger are. He recognised the existence of non-practical emotions and was prepared to include them within the alogical half of the soul. An important example is shame. In the *Ethics* Aristotle attributes this emotion to man's alogical side and treats it briefly after he has run through the several moral virtues. He hesitates as to whether it is an emotion or a disposition and concludes that it is more an emotion than a disposition (1128ᵇ10–15). For our purposes the important point is that a man may feel ashamed and yet do nothing at all. If he is ashamed of some past deed, it may be simply too late to undo things or even make amends. In such a case a person merely suffers and perhaps turns red (1128ᵇ13). In extreme cases an ashamed man may commit suicide, but in doing this he is not rectifying the past. When, for example, Ajax comes to his senses and realises that he has slaughtered animals, he feels humiliated and calls for his own death (Soph., *Aj.* 361, 7). The chorus warns that he is only adding to his own misery and asks why he is tormented by past deeds when they cannot be undone (363, 377–8). The feeling of Ajax is understandable, but so is the attitude of the chorus. When deeds are beyond remedy, there may be nothing which an ashamed man can or ought to do.

This is not to say that shame is of no importance in regard to good behaviour. In Plato's *Laws* the Athenian Stranger is explicit concerning the value of shame and the great evil of shamelessness (*Laws* 647ᵃ8–ᵇ1). In the *Rhetoric* Aristotle recognises the importance of shame as a check upon unworthy desires and cites the well-known admission of Alcaeus: 'I wish to say something, but shame restrains me' (1367ᵃ10–11). In the *Ethics* Aristotle is equally clear concerning the restraining influence of shame. Children, he tells us, ought to have a sense of shame, for they live by emotion and are prevented from error by shame (1128ᵇ16–18; cf. 1179ᵇ11). In regard to military dangers shame is even spoken of as a virtue, for it helps restrain citizens from ignoble flight (1116ᵃ27–9). But despite these useful effects of feeling shame, it is true that shame is not logically tied to action of any particular kind and that Aristotle is on solid ground when he defines shame simply as a pain or disturbance concerning bad things which appear likely to involve us in discredit (*Rhet.* 1383ᵇ12–14). Shame is not a practical emotion, so that neither a goal nor an action is mentioned in its essential definition.

Indignation is another example of a non-practical emotion. Aristotle is explicit concerning the cognitive nature of this emotion. He ties indignation to the thought of unmerited good fortune (*Rhet.* 1386ᵇ11, 1387ᵃ9) and so makes clear that a man feels indignant when he deems another's success unmerited. Aristotle is also clear that this emotion need not be manifested in action. An indignant man may, for example, be disturbed because a newly-rich person has attained a high office (*Rhet.* 1387ᵃ22–3). He feels indignant at an accomplished fact which cannot be undone. He wishes that things were otherwise, but he does not act for an impossible goal. This is not to say that an indignant man never exhibits his emotion in some goal-directed action. Clearly there are occasions when indignation may lead to attempts at rectification. But it is to say that the emotion of indignation is not logically tied to some goal for which the indignant man always acts. Indignation is compatible with inaction. Aristotle is alert to this and therefore recognises that indignation does not invite moral virtue in the sense of a practical disposition involving choice. Of course, Aristotle recognises that indignation at unmerited good fortune may be said to manifest good character (*Rhet.* 1386ᵇ11–12). But he does not develop a moral virtue of righteous indignation. His investigation of emotional response had made clear that indignation is a non-practical emotion and therefore poor material for a practical disposition involving choice and goal-directed action.

An interesting consequence of all this is that we can see a conceptual reason why Aristotle had no moral virtue corresponding to the Christian virtue of mercy. Being merciful is tied to the emotion of pity (*eleos*, cf. *Matt.* 5.7, 9.13; *Heb.* 2.17, 4.16; *Tilt.* 3.5) and feeling pity is for Aristotle compatible with doing nothing. He defines pity without mentioning a particular mode of action (*Rhet.* 1385ᵇ13–16) and includes among the objects of pity such irremediable items as death, age and ugliness (1386ᵃ8, 11). Apparently, Aristotle viewed pity as a non-practical emotion and therefore as an emotion that does not invite virtue in the sense of a practical disposition to choose and act. Of course, such a conceptual explanation may not be the entire story. Among Greeks so concerned with personal worth as to value magnanimity (*megalopsychia*, cf. *EN* 1123ᵃ34–25ᵃ35) and so thorough in hatred as to see nothing wrong with delighting in the misfortune of one's enemies (cf. Plato. *Phil.* 49ᵈ3–4), mercy would seem to be an odd virtue. But it should be clearly observed that Aristotle groups pity together with indignation and attributes both to good character (*Rhet.* 1386ᵇ8–12). Aristotle himself might well have endorsed the spirit of the fifth Beatitude: Blessed are the merciful (*eleêmones*) for they shall obtain mercy (*Matt.* 5.7), and still objected to a moral virtue of mercy on conceptual grounds.

5. Temperance and human appetites

Aristotle's investigation of emotion made him alert not only to an important difference between practical and non-practical emotions but also to an equally important difference between emotions and bodily drives. He recognised that the efficient cause of an emotion is some thought or belief, while the efficient cause of a bodily drive is some physiological change or disturbance. What interests us is that Aristotle recognised such a fundamental difference between emotions and bodily drives and yet was moved neither to exclude hunger, thirst and sexual desire from the sphere of ethical concern nor to refuse temperance the status of moral virtue. Instead he followed the Athenian Stranger in recognising the importance of appetites like hunger, thirst and sexual desire (Plato, *Laws* 782ᵈ10–783ᵇ1), extended the alogical half of the soul to include the biological faculty of nutrition (1102ᵃ32–3) and connected temperance with natural desires for nourishment and sexual intercourse (1118ᵇ9–11). This is especially striking since Aristotle also followed the Athenian Stranger (*Laws* 782ᵉ2–3) in recognising explicitly that such needs are not peculiar to human beings. In the *Politics*, he tells us that the urge to reproduce does not originate in choice but is present naturally in plants and animals (1252^a28–30). In the *Ethics* he says that the nutritive faculty is present in all nurtured and growing things including embryos. It is said to be active during sleep and to have no part in human virtue (1102^a32–$^b12$). This is quite intelligible. Nutritive processes are not themselves actions, and when they are the cause of behaviour, we are likely to explain the behaviour by reference to bodily phenomena and to distinguish the behaviour from action for which a man is responsible. In other words, we recognise that a man's physiological constitution may affect his behaviour in ways that are important but not normally praised or blamed. Fluidity of marrow and porosity of bone, for example, may be on occasion solely or primarily responsible for sexual excess, and when they are, then Timaios would seem to be correct in holding that the excess is a disease that calls for treatment and not censure (Plato, *Tim.* 86^c3–$^e3$).[1]

Still, the fact that bodily conditions and bodily drives are not in themselves subject to moral praise or blame, does not mean that the hunger, thirst, and sexual desire of human beings cannot be related to moral virtue (cf. Plato, *Laws* 782^d11) and that Aristotle is necessarily confused in developing a theory of moral virtue around emotions like anger and fear and at the same time treating temperance as a moral virtue connected with bodily pleasures and the sense of touch common to all animals (1118^a2, $^b1$). We should remember that Aristotle is careful to distinguish between rational and non-rational appetites. The former are attributed to persuasion, while the latter are said to originate through the body and not to result from judgment (*Rhet.* 1370^a19–25). What interests us is not so much that Aristotle assigns hunger, thirst, and sexual desire to the class of non-rational appetites (1370^a22–3) as that he recognises the possibility of other appetites which are acquired through persuasion. In other words, Aristotle opens the door to desires which are concerned with bodily pleasures and yet are different from hunger, thirst, and sexual desire conceived of as non-rational

[1] A qualification is necessary. While disease itself demands treatment and invites pity, men are expected to respond to disease in fitting ways. In the *Ethics* Aristotle says that disease ought not to be feared (1115^a17) and in the *Politics* he tells us that a morally good man handles disease in a noble manner (1332^a19–20; cf. Plato, *Laws* 632^a5–$^b1$).

appetites caused by physiological changes.[1] Bodily pleasures may be the object of acquired desires whose efficient cause is cognitive and open to reasoned persuasion. The application of all this to ethics and moral virtue should be clear enough. The temperate man is disposed to desire the right bodily pleasures on the right occasion, not because his bodily processes have developed some miraculous rhythm, but rather because he has been through moral *paideia* and so acquired loves and hates which are rational appetites obedient to reasoned argument. Hence, Aristotle does not hesitate to group habituation in regard to bodily pleasures together with habituation in regard to fear and anger (1103^b13-22, 1104^a33-^b3). Like courage and good temper, temperance is thought of as a learned disposition to evaluate properly particular situations and to manifest proper evaluation in appropriate behaviour. The temperate man feels disgust at unseemly pleasures (1119^a13), not because he has a weak stomach but because he has been properly educated.[2] Having acquired a noble goal (1119^b9) and having learned to delight in avoiding unseemly pleasures (1104^b5-6), the temperate man differs from the intemperate man who thinks that he ought to pursue pleasure (1152^a5) and therefore selects pleasures in preference to other things (1119^a1-3). Temperate men are very different from intemperate men, but they share at least one thing in common. Both are characterised by cognitive dispositions which go well beyond the capacities of animals. About this Aristotle is quite clear. Animals can be temperate and intemperate only in a metaphorical sense (1149^b31-2). In contrast, human beings can be

---

[1] Aristotle does not deny that hunger, thirst and sexual desire conceived of as non-rational appetites may be the occasion for considerable thought by human beings. For example, a hungry man often thinks about his gnawing stomach; he may report to others that his stomach is empty and he may judge that this food is more filling than that food. But this kind of involvement of cognition in cases of human hunger, thirst and sexual desire does not tell against the essential difference Aristotle sees between non-rational and rational appetite. At least Aristotle would insist that the efficient cause of non-rational appetites remains bodily (when a man thinks and says that his stomach is empty, he is focusing upon and reporting the cause of his appetite; he is not causing the appetite) and therefore serves to maintain an essential difference between non-rational appetites and rational appetites whose efficient cause is a learned judgment.

[2] Cf. 1179^b29-31 where Aristotle is concerned with training youth so that they love the noble and are disgusted by the shameful. Here as at 1119^a13 feeling disgust (*dyscherainein*) is making an unfavourable assessment.

educated and therefore are capable of temperance and intemperance in the unqualified sense of human moral virtue and vice.[1]

It seems, then, that the loves and hates of a temperate man are quite different from hunger, thirst, and sexual desire conceived of as non-rational appetites common to men and animals. The former are acquired and involve judgment as their efficient cause. The latter are innate and do not involve judgment as their efficient cause. This means that on occasion temperance will demand 'sitting on' one's desire for food, drink or sex. When, for example, an empty stomach causes acute hunger, persuasion will be as ineffective as it is in regard to simple sensations of heat (1113^b26-30). A man either fills his stomach or manfully controls his urge to eat. He does not reason his hunger away. Still, it would be a mistake to think that temperance is a continual struggle between bodily drives and acquired loves and hates. As previously pointed out (Chapter Three, Section 1), the habituation of young persons may include more than a training in values. By withholding himself from bodily pleasures (1104^a33-4, $^b5-6$) a youth or even a mature person may learn not only to despise excessive indulgence but also to ignore bodily discomforts. Indeed, by repeated acts of self-discipline he may even effect a welcome bodily alteration. He may,

---

[1] The Nicomachean account of temperance shows considerable Platonic influence (see my 'Aristotle: Animals' 147). The mention of the *epithymêtikon* and psychic symphony recalls tripartition, several passages in the *Topics* (123^a34, 136^b13, 138^b2, 139^b33) and Plato's *Republic* where temperance in the individual is construed as a symphony within the tripartite soul (442^c10-^d1; cf. 430^e3). Although Aristotle is beyond tripartition, the connection of temperance with the *epithymêtikon* is not just an unfortunate lapse into Platonism. Since the *epithymêtikon* (or at least the *epithymêtikon* as presented in the *Republic*) is the seat not only of bodily drives but also of certain emotions and cognitions (see above Chapter Two, Sections 3 and 4), it is natural enough to connect it with temperance conceived of as a disposition to assess and respond to bodily pleasures. In other words, the *epithymêtikon* can make room for both the bodily-sensitive and also the cognitive elements of temperance. What the *epithymêtikon* cannot make room for is the *logos* which is said to be in symphony with the *epithymêtikon* of the temperate man (1119^b15-16). But then neither can the *alogon* of bipartition. Both the *epithymêtikon* and the *alogon* are without calculative and deliberative functions. But both are cognitive and can be associated with certain opinions or assessments which agree with those arrived at by reasoned reflection. It would seem, then, that Aristotle is not making a serious mistake when he slides into Platonic terminology and speaks of the *epithymêtikon* in symphony with *logos*. He could restate his point in terms of bipartition but does not do so in this 'Platonic' portion of the *Ethics*.

for example, shrink his stomach and thereby eliminate the agony of repeated bouts with gnawing hunger. Furthermore, it is all too easy to exaggerate the importance of bodily drives in determining human behaviour. As already mentioned (Chapter Two, Section 3) Plato classified *erôs* together with fear and anger as mixed pleasures and pains of the soul itself (*Phil.* 47ᵉ1). This is not foolishness. The sexual desire (not to say love) of human beings is often caused by thoughts and beliefs.[1] Just as anger is caused and given direction by the thought that someone has committed an outrage, so sexual desire may be awakened and directed by the thought that someone is beautiful and worth having. In such cases judgment arouses the body and not vice versa. Of course, there are cases in which it may be difficult to decide which comes first. But on closer inspection this difficulty may be a mark of similarity between human sexual desire and an emotion such as anger. For in the case of anger bodily and cognitive factors may interact quite closely. At least Aristotle holds that bodily conditions actually predispose a person to anger (*De An.* 403ᵃ21–4) and that there is a significant correlation between youth and angry emotion (*Rhet.* 1369ᵃ9, 1389ᵃ9).[2] Similarly he recognises that youth predisposes a person to appetitive behaviour (*Rhet.* 1369ᵃ9–10, 1389ᵃ3–9), and might argue that as in the case of anger so in certain cases of sexual desire this bodily condition is a predisposition and not the efficient cause which is more often than realised some cognitive judgment. Of course, Aristotle never tries to convert all instances of appetition into emotional responses, but perhaps we can conclude that his work on emotion may have helped him to appreciate the complexity and variety of human appetite and in any event did help him to see how moral virtue can be related to appetite without becoming a blind habit more appropriate to animal than to human behaviour.

6. *Non-emotional modes of social interaction*

Finally we should consider three exceptional moral virtues whose treatment shows, I think, considerable sophistication on the part

---

[1] It is difficult to be certain what English word properly translates *erôs* at *Phil.* 47ᵉ1, but it is interesting that modern philosophers are not averse to treating love as a cognitive emotion parallel to anger. Cf. most recently R. Solomon, 'Emotions and Choice', *The Review of Metaphysics* 27 (1973) 25, 27, 39–40.

[2] On fear see above, p. 34 n.1.

of Aristotle. These three virtues are friendliness, wittiness and truthfulness. What especially interests us is that Aristotle associates these moral virtues neither with emotions nor with appetites. Instead he groups them together under the label of virtues concerned with human relations in speech and action (1108ª11, 1126ᵇ11–12, 1127ª20, 24, 1128ᵇ5–6). What Aristotle has in mind when he joins speech to action is not immediately obvious and perhaps confusing because of earlier associations of speech with action. In the *Iliad*, for example, Homer makes Phoinix say that he was sent to Peleus to teach Achilles to be a speaker of words and a doer of deeds (9.442–3). Similarly in Plato's *Protagoras* the great sophist claims to teach *euboulia* with a resultant ability to act and speak in public matters (319ª2, cf. 326ᵇ4). In his *History* Thucydides describes Pericles as most able to speak and act (1.139.4) and in the *Anabasis* Xenophon has the Spartan Cheirisophos praise him for what he says and does (3.1.45). Clearly the excellence that Phoinix and Protagoras claim to teach and that Pericles and Xenophon are said to possess cannot be identified easily with one or all of those virtues that Aristotle groups together as mean-dispositions in speech and action. Phoinix is not teaching friendliness, wittiness and truthfulness but rather how to speak in debate and to act in war (9.440–1). Moreover, in the sixth book of the *Ethics* deliberative excellence (*euboulia*) is treated among the virtues of the logical half of the soul (1140ª26, 1141ᵇ8–14, 1142ª31–ᵇ33) and Pericles is introduced in conjunction with practical wisdom, not moral virtue (1140ᵇ8). In contrast friendliness, wittiness and truthfulness are treated as moral virtues. They are dissociated from emotion, but still count as perfections of the alogical half.

The dissociation of friendliness, wittiness and truthfulness from emotional response is intelligible enough. Consider truthfulness. This disposition is not closely connected with an emotion in the way that, say, good temper is connected with anger. Of course, there is no conceptual absurdity in an emotion concerned with true and false assertions. But if such an emotion is logically possible, it is also generally ignored and does not seem to have attracted a name either in Greek or in English. Aristotle was prepared to invent names (cf. 1108ª16–19), but he does not do so in this case, partly or even primarily because he does not think of truthfulness as a disposition tied to emotional response. This is not to overlook the fact that the truthfulness with which Aristotle concerns himself is not truthfulness in general but rather truthfulness in regard to assessments of oneself (1127ᵃ23–6). Aristotle is concerned with a disposition which he describes as nameless and lying mid-way between boastfulness and irony (1127ᵃ13–14). This means that Aristotle conceives of truthfulness in a sense narrower than we might at first suspect. But this does not affect the basic point that truthfulness is not closely tied to emotional response. Being truthful is not a matter of feeling veracious on the right occasions but rather a matter of owning up to what is actually possessed (1127ᵃ25).[1]

The same may be the case with friendliness and wittiness. The virtue of friendliness, Aristotle tells us, has never been given a name. It is like friendship but differs in that it involves no emotion or affection for those with whom one associates. It is not because he loves or hates, responds emotionally out of love or hate, that the man possessing this unnamed virtue takes everything in the right way, but rather because he is the kind of man he is (1126ᵇ19–25). That is to say he is disposed to do whatever he does in a friendly manner quite apart from feelings or emotions of personal affection. Similarly if wittiness or *eutrapelia* is thought of as a kind of charming versatility, it, too, may be manifested in various ways that do not involve emotional response. A man whose playful manner is always in good taste is, so to speak, well-turned (1128ᵃ10) and dexterous (1128ᵃ17). He has the sort of disposition which marks off an attractive doctor from an unattractive one whose dour manner is repulsive to healthy and sick persons alike (Hipp., *Decorum* 7). A pleasing bedside manner is important for a good relationship between doctor and patient, but it is not normally exhibited in emotional response. Rather it seems to be manifested in the way a doctor deals professionally with patients and may be thought of as a particular instance of the tactful dexterity Pericles thought characterised his fellow citizens (Thuc. 2.41.1).[2]

[1] See F. Dirlmeier, *Aristoteles, Eudemische Ethik* (Berlin 1962) 351 and also E. Bedford ('Emotions', 294, reprint 90) who seems to be influenced by Aristotle when he argues that the overlap between virtues and emotions is not complete and that veracity is a virtue not connected with an emotion.

[2] It is, of course, possible to construe *eutrapelia* differently, so that it is connected with the emotion of finding something funny. For a fuller account of *eutrapelia* in connection with jeering abuse and thinking oneself superior, see my 'Questionable Mean-Dispositions' 216–19. Dirlmeier (*Eudemische* 351, 355) points out a connection between *eutrapelia* and emotion but seems to err in his treatment of *Rhet.* 1389ᵇ11–12 and in suggesting that emotional

At this point it may be asked why wittiness, friendliness and truthfulness are regarded as perfections of man's alogical half. If these three dispositions are not tied directly to either emotions or appetites, why are they grouped together with the moral virtues of courage, good temper and temperance? Wittiness, for example, might be thought of as some kind of knack quite distinct from moral character. It might be thought of as an ability or skill which is like a *techne* in being compatible with voluntary mistakes (1140ᵇ23) and with ulterior motives of the worst kind. Furthermore, wittiness might seem to be equally at home within the logical half of the soul. At least, Isocrates recognises a close connection between *eutrapelia* and oratory (*Antidosis* 296), and we can speak of dexterity and wittiness in discourse and deliberation and therefore in exercises of the logical half of the soul. The difficulty here is, I think, only apparent. For Aristotle the mean-dispositions of wittiness, friendliness and truthfulness involve learned attitudes and goals and are exercised only when a man does what he does because it is right and noble to do so. Friendliness as a moral virtue is never simply doing whatever one does in a pleasant manner. Unlike the obsequious man who thinks he ought to avoid giving pain to whomever he meets (1126ᵇ13–14), the friendly man considers what is noble and beneficial (1126ᵇ29) and on occasion chooses to give pain rather than pleasure (1126ᵇ33). Similarly the truthful man is not adequately or fully described as the man who neither exaggerates nor understates the qualities he possesses. Falsehood is base and deserves censure, truth is noble and deserves praise (1127ᵃ28–30). The truthful man has learned this and therefore loves the truth (1127ᵇ4) and avoids falsehood as something shameful (1127ᵇ5–6). Finally the witty man is not marked simply by a continuous wit and charming manner. In contrast with the buffoon who aims at raising a laugh (1128ᵃ6), the *eutrapelos* is concerned with saying whatever befits a good and free man (1128ᵃ17–19). In short, he is an educated man (1128ᵃ21) who has been taught to value proper speech and to manifest this value in tactful and versatile wit.

It appears that friendliness, truthfulness and wittiness are classified as moral virtues of man's alogical side, because like all

responses in general and the laughing responses of young persons in particular lack an intellectual or cognitive element. When young people break out in laughter they are expressing an educated *hybris* (*Rhet.* 1389ᵇ12) which involves thinking oneself superior (*Rhet.* 1378ᵇ27–9).

moral virtues they involve a learned disposition to make certain kinds of assessments and to do what one does because it is right and noble. This is hardly surprising, if we keep in mind that a person's alogical side is the concern of the early *paideia* or moral training carried on through music and dance and other means capable of instilling moral principles and habituating young people to act in accordance with their principles. Since young people live primarily in accordance with their passions and desires (1095^{a}4, 1119^{b}5–6), the early *paideia* focuses on emotions and appetites and tries to develop good dispositions such as courage, good temper and temperance. Such dispositions may be considered of especial importance, but they are not all there is to a good *êthos*. Just as legislators may concern themselves with what people say to one another (cf. 1128^{a}30–1) so educators cannot afford to neglect the way people interact. Proper modes of social interaction are to be taught to young persons, so that they come to know and to value positively good manners. Young persons cannot be expected to explain why truth is noble and praiseworthy (1127^{a}28–30), for reasoned explanations belong to the logical half of the soul which develops later in life. But they can come to believe that truth is noble and to love truth itself, for their alogical side is open to moral *paideia*.

Perhaps we may conclude that Aristotle's analysis of moral virtue shows him at his best. It exhibits not only a keen interest in emotional response but also a philosophical control of considerable merit. When Aristotle seeks to elucidate the nature of moral virtue, his initial move is to introduce emotions (1105^{b}19–23) and to develop a conception of human virtue (1102^{a}14) which excludes animals lacking the capacity of emotional response. But for all his interest in emotional response Aristotle does not lose sight of the fact that the sphere of moral virtue goes beyond emotions like anger and fear. He acknowledges the importance of temperance and is even prepared to recognise truthfulness, wittiness and friendliness as moral virtues. This is a mark of mature philosophical thought.[1]

[1] And a mark which distinguishes the *Nichomachean Ethics* from the *Eudemian Ethics*. The latter work does not exhibit the Nicomachean sophistication. It treats not only truthfulness, wittiness and friendliness but also dignity as emotional mean-dispositions. This is a mistake which at best may serve to underline the importance of emotion within the alogical half conceived of as the sphere of moral virtue. Of course, *eutrapelia* can be construed narrowly, so that it is connected with the emotion of finding something funny or laughable. A witty man may be regarded as one who enjoys a good sense of humour and

Aristotle has so thoroughly investigated emotions that he knows what they can and cannot do. He is able to recognise their central importance without thinking that they exhaust the sphere of moral virtue.

---

therefore responds properly to the laughable and in particular to jeering abuse (see above, p. 89 n. 2). Perhaps friendliness can be reinterpreted to remove the Nicomachean restriction against feelings of affection (1126ᵇ22–5), but the *Eudemian Ethics* does not spell out how it proposes to connect friendliness with emotion. Neither does it spell out how truthfulness is to be connected with emotional response. Here silence may be a confession of inability. For truthfulness is not connected readily with an emotion, and we may wonder whether truthfulness and also friendliness and wittiness together with dignity ought to be grouped alongside of righteous indignation and shame under the label *pathêtikai mesotêtes* (1233ᵇ18). There may be no difficulty in relating righteous indignation and shame to a *pathos* (1234ᵃ27), but there certainly is a serious difficulty in the cases of truthfulness and dignity. It looks as if the *Eudemian Ethics* is forcing these mean-dispositions into a preconceived framework. Of course, no chronological conclusions can be drawn. It may be that dispositions like truthfulness and dignity are lumped together with emotional dispositions because the *Eudemian Ethics* was composed at a time when the distinction between reasoning and emotional response was still fresh, exciting and in need of further refinement. Alternatively it may be that some later Peripatetic did not understand or care about the details of bipartition and grasping only the fundamental opposition between reasoning and emotion forced the label *pathêtikai mesotêtes* on dispositions such as truthfulness and dignity.

INDEX OF MODERN AUTHORS